W9-AEQ-254

VIRTUE AND TERROR

This essential new series features classic texts by key figures that took center stage during a period of insurrection. Each book is introduced by a major contemporary radical writer who shows how these incendiary words still have the power to inspire, to provoke and maybe to ignite new revolutions . . .

VIRTUE
AND TERROR

◆

MAXIMILIEN ROBESPIERRE

INTRODUCTION BY SLAVOJ ŽIŽEK

TEXTS SELECTED AND ANNOTATED BY JEAN DUCANGE
TRANSLATION BY JOHN HOWE

VERSO
London • New York

First published by Verso 2007
© Verso 2007
Translation © John Howe 2007
Introduction © Slavoj Žižek 2007
All rights reserved

3 5 7 9 10 8 6 4 2

Verso
UK: 6 Meard Street, London W1F 0EG
USA: 20 Jay Street, Brooklyn, NY, 11201
www.versobooks.com

Verso is the imprint of New Left Books

ISBN-13: 978-1-84467-584-5

British Library Cataloguing in Publication Data
A catalogue record for this book is available from the British Library

Library of Congress Cataloging-in-Publication Data
A catalog record for this book is available from the Library of Congress

Typeset in Bembo by Hewer Text UK Ltd, Edinburgh
Printed in the USA by Quebecor World, Fairfield

CONTENTS

INTRODUCTION

ROBESPIERRE, OR, THE 'DIVINE VIOLENCE' OF TERROR

Slavoj Žižek

When, in 1953, Zhou Enlai, the Chinese Prime Minister, was in Geneva for the peace negotiations to end the Korean War, a French journalist asked him what he thought about the French Revolution; Zhou replied: 'It is still too early to tell.' In a way, he was right: with the disintegration of the 'people's democracies' in the late 1990s, the struggle for the historical significance of the French Revolution flared up again. The liberal revisionists tried to impose the notion that the demise of Communism in 1989 occurred at exactly the right moment: it marked the end of the era which began in 1789, the final failure of the statist-revolutionary model which first entered the scene with the Jacobins.

Nowhere is the dictum 'every history is a history of the present' more true than in the case of the French Revolution: its historiographical reception always closely mirrored the twists and turns of political struggles. The identifying mark of all kinds of conservatives is its flat rejection: the French Revolution was a catastrophe from its very beginning, the product of the godless modern mind; it is to be interpreted as God's punishment for the humanity's wicked ways, so its traces should be undone as thoroughly as possible. The typical liberal attitude is a differentiated one: its formula is '1789 without 1793'. In short, what the sensitive liberals want is a decaffeinated revolution, a revolution which doesn't smell of revolution. François Furet and others thus try to deprive the French Revolution of its status as the founding event of modern democracy, relegating it to a historical anomaly: there was a historical necessity to assert the modern principles of personal freedom, etc., but, as the English example demonstrates, the same could have been much more effectively achieved in a more peaceful way . . . Radicals are, on the contrary, possessed by what Alain Badiou called the 'passion of the Real': if you say A – equality, human rights and freedoms – you should not shirk from its consequences but muster the courage to say B – the terror needed to really defend and assert the A.[1]

However, it is all too easy to say that today's Left should simply continue along this path. Something, some kind of historical cut, effectively took place in 1990: everyone, today's 'radical Left' included, is somehow ashamed of the Jacobin legacy of revolutionary terror with its state-centralized character, so that the commonly accepted motto is that the Left, if it is to regain political effectiveness, should thoroughly reinvent itself, finally abandoning the so-called 'Jacobin paradigm'. In our post-modern era of 'emergent properties', the chaotic interaction of multiple subjectivities, free interaction rather than centralized hierarchy, the multitude of opinions instead of one Truth, the Jacobin dictatorship is fundamentally 'not to our taste' (the term 'taste' should be given all its historical weight, as the name for a basic ideological disposition). Can one imagine something more foreign to our universe of the freedom of opinions, of market competition, of nomadic pluralist interaction, etc., than Robespierre's politics of Truth (with a capital T, of course), whose proclaimed goal is 'to return the destiny of liberty into the hands of the truth'? Such a Truth can only be enforced in a terrorist manner:

> If the mainspring of popular government in peacetime is virtue, the mainspring of popular government in revolution is both virtue and terror: virtue, without which terror is disastrous; terror, without which virtue is powerless. Terror is nothing but prompt, severe, inflexible justice; it is therefore an emanation of virtue; it is not so much a specific principle as a consequence of the general principle of democracy applied to our homeland's most pressing needs.[2]

Robespierre's line of argumentation reaches its climax in the paradoxical identification of the opposites: revolutionary terror 'sublates' the opposition between punishment and clemency – the just and severe punishment of the enemies *is* the highest form of clemency, so that, in it, rigour and charity coincide:

> To punish the oppressors of humanity: that is clemency; to forgive them is barbarity. The rigour of tyrants has that rigour as its sole principle: that of the republican government is based on beneficence.[3]

What, then, should those who remain faithful to the legacy of the radical Left do with all this? Two things, at least. First, the terrorist past has to be accepted as *ours*, even – or precisely because – it is critically rejected. The only alternative to the half-hearted defensive position of feeling guilty in front of our liberal or Rightist critics is: we have to do the critical job better than our opponents. This, however, is not the entire story: one should also not allow our opponents to determine the field and topic of the struggle. What this means is that the ruthless self-critique should go hand in hand with a fearless admission of what, to paraphrase Marx's judgement on Hegel's dialectics, one is tempted to call the 'rational kernel' of the Jacobin Terror:

> Materialist dialectics assumes, without particular joy, that, till now, no political subject was able to arrive at the eternity of the truth it was deploying without moments of terror. Since, as Saint-Just asked: 'What do those who want neither Virtue nor Terror want?' His answer is well-known: they want corruption – another name for the subject's defeat.[4]

Or, as Saint-Just put it succinctly: 'That which produces the general good is always terrible.'[5] These words should not be interpreted as a warning against the temptation to impose violently the general good onto a society, but, on the contrary, as a bitter truth to be fully endorsed.

The further crucial point to bear in mind is that, for Robespierre, revolutionary terror is the very opposite of war: Robespierre was a pacifist, not out of hypocrisy or humanitarian sensitivity, but because he was well aware that war *among* nations as a rule serves as the means to obfuscate revolutionary struggle *within* each nation. Robespierre's speech 'On the War' is of special importance today: it shows him as a true pacifist who forcefully denounces the patriotic call to war, even if the war is formulated as the defence of the Revolution, as the attempt of those who want 'revolution without a revolution' to divert the radicalization of the revolutionary process. His stance is thus the exact opposite of those who need war to militarize social life and take dictatorial control over it.[6]

Which is why Robespierre also denounced the temptation to export revolution to other countries, forcefully 'liberating' them:

> The French are not afflicted with a mania for rendering any nation happy and free against its will. All the kings could have vegetated or died unpunished on their blood-spattered thrones, if they had been able to respect the French people's independence.[7]

The Jacobin revolutionary terror is sometimes (half) justified as the 'founding crime' of the bourgeois universe of law and order, in which citizens are allowed to pursue their interests in peace. One should reject this claim on two counts. Not only is it factually wrong (many conservatives were quite right to point out that one can achieve bourgeois law and order also without terrorist excesses, as was the case in Great Britain – although there is the case of Cromwell . . .); much more important, the revolutionary Terror of 1792-94 was not a case of what Walter Benjamin and others call state-founding violence, but a case of 'divine violence'.[8] Interpreters of Benjamin struggle with what 'divine violence' might effectively mean – is it yet another Leftist dream of a 'pure' event which never really takes place? One should recall here Friedrich Engels's reference to the Paris Commune as an example of the dictatorship of the proletariat:

> Of late, the Social-Democratic philistine has once more been filled with wholesome terror at the words: Dictatorship of the Proletariat. Well and good, gentlemen, do you want to know what this dictatorship looks like? Look at the Paris Commune. That was the Dictatorship of the Proletariat.[9]

One should repeat this, *mutatis mutandis*, apropos divine violence: 'Well and good, gentlemen critical theorists, do you want to know what this divine violence looks like? Look at the revolutionary Terror of 1792-94. That was the Divine Violence.' (And the series goes on: the Red Terror of 1919 . . .) That is to say, one should fearlessly identify divine violence with a positively existing historical phenomenon, thus avoiding all obscurantist mystification. When those outside the structured social field strike 'blindly', demanding *and* enacting immediate justice/vengeance, this is 'divine violence' – recall, a decade or so ago, the panic in Rio de Janeiro when crowds descended from the *favelas* into the rich part of the city and started looting and burning supermarkets – *this* was 'divine violence' . . . Like the biblical locusts, the divine punishment for men's sinful ways, it strikes out of nowhere, a means without end – or, as Robespierre put it in his speech in which he demanded the execution of Louis XVI:

> Peoples do not judge in the same way as courts of law; they do not hand down sentences, they throw thunderbolts; they do not condemn kings, they drop them back into the void; and this justice is worth just as much as that of the courts.[10]

The Benjaminian 'divine violence' should be thus conceived as divine in the precise sense of the old Latin motto *vox populi, vox dei: not* in the perverse sense of 'we are doing it as mere instruments of the People's Will', but as the heroic assumption of the solitude of a sovereign decision. It is a decision (to kill, to risk or lose one's own life) made in absolute solitude, not covered by the big Other. If it is extra-moral, it is not 'immoral', it does not give the agent the licence to kill mindlessly with some kind of angelic innocence. The motto of divine violence is *fiat iustitia, pereat mundus*: it is *justice*, the point of non-distinction between justice and vengeance, in which the 'people' (the anonymous part of no-part) imposes its terror and makes other parts pay the price – the Judgement Day for the long history of oppression, exploitation, suffering – or, as Robespierre himself put it in a poignant way:

> What do you want, you who would like truth to be powerless on the lips of representatives of the French people? Truth undoubtedly has its power, it has its anger, its own despotism; it has touching accents and terrible ones, that resound with force in pure hearts as in guilty consciences, and that untruth can no more imitate than Salome can imitate the thunderbolts of heaven; but accuse nature of it, accuse the people, which wants it and loves it.[11]

And this is what Robespierre aims at in his famous accusation to the moderates that what they really want is a 'revolution without a revolution': they want a revolution deprived of the excess in which democracy and terror coincide, a revolution respecting social rules, subordinated to pre-existing norms, a revolution in which violence is deprived of the 'divine' dimension and thus reduced to a strategic intervention serving precise and limited goals:

Citizens, did you want a revolution without a revolution? What is this spirit of persecution that has come to revise, so to speak, the one that broke our chains? But what sure judgement can one make of the effects that can follow these great commotions? Who can mark, after the event, the exact point at which the waves of popular insurrection should break? At that price, what people could ever have shaken off the yoke of despotism? For while it is true that a great nation cannot rise in a simultaneous movement, and that tyranny can only be hit by the portion of citizens that is closest to it, how would these ever dare to attack it if, after the victory, delegates from remote parts could hold them responsible for the duration or violence of the political torment that had saved the homeland? They ought to be regarded as justified by tacit proxy for the whole of society. The French, friends of liberty, meeting in Paris last August, acted in that role, in the name of all the departments. They should either be approved or repudiated entirely. To make them criminally responsible for a few apparent or real disorders, inseparable from so great a shock, would be to punish them for their devotion.[12]

This authentic revolutionary logic can be discerned already at the level of rhetorical figures, where Robespierre likes to turn around the standard procedure of first evoking an apparently 'realist' position and then displaying its illusory nature: he often starts with presenting a position or a description of a situation as absurd exaggeration, fiction, and then goes on to remind us that what, in a first approach, cannot but appear as a fiction, is actually truth itself: 'But what am I saying? What I have just presented as an absurd hypothesis is actually a very certain reality.' It is this radical revolutionary stance which also enables Robespierre to denounce the 'humanitarian' concern with victims of the revolutionary 'divine violence':

A sensibility that wails almost exclusively over the enemies of liberty seems suspect to me. Stop shaking the tyrant's bloody robe in my face, or I will believe that you wish to put Rome in chains.[13]

The critical analysis and the acceptance of the historical legacy of the Jacobins overlap in the real question that should be discussed: does the (often deplorable) actuality of the revolutionary terror compel us to reject the very idea of Terror, or is there a way to *repeat* it in today's different historical constellation, to redeem its virtual content from its actualization? It *can* and *should* be done, and the most concise formula of repeating the event designated by the name 'Robespierre' is: to pass from (Robespierre's) humanist terror to anti-humanist (or, rather, inhuman) terror.

In his *Le siècle*, Alain Badiou argues that the shift from 'humanism *and* terror' to 'humanism *or* terror' that occurred towards the end of the twentieth century was a sign of political regression. In 1946, Maurice Merleau-Ponty wrote *Humanism and Terror*, his defence of Soviet Communism as involving a kind of Pascalean wager that announces the topic of what Bernard Williams later developed as the notion of 'moral luck': the present terror will be retroactively justified if the society that emerges from it proves to be truly human; today, such a conjunction of terror and humanism is properly unthinkable, the predominant liberal view replaces *and* with *or*: either humanism or terror . . . More precisely, there are four variations on this motif: humanism *and* terror, humanism *or* terror, each either in a 'positive' or in a 'negative' sense. 'Humanism and terror' in a positive sense is what Merleau-Ponty elaborated, it sustains Stalinism (the forceful – 'terrorist' – engendering of the New Man), and is already clearly discernible in the French Revolution, in the guise of Robespierre's conjunction of virtue and terror. This conjunction can be negated in two ways. It can involve the choice 'humanism *or* terror,' i.e., the liberal-humanist project in all its versions, from dissident anti-Stalinist humanism up to today's neo-Habermassians (Luc Ferry and Alain Renaut in France, for example) and other defenders of human rights *against* (totalitarian, fundamentalist) terror. Or it can retain the conjunction 'humanism *and* terror,' but in a negative mode: all those philosophical and ideological orientations, from Heidegger and conservative Christians to partisans of Oriental spirituality and deep ecology, who perceive terror as the truth – the ultimate consequence – of the humanist project itself, of its *hubris*.

There is, however, a fourth variation, usually left aside: the choice 'humanism *or* terror', but with *terror*, not humanism, as a positive term. This is a radical position difficult to sustain, but, perhaps, our only hope: it does not amount to the obscene madness of openly pursuing a 'terrorist and inhuman politics', but something much more difficult to think through. In today's 'post-deconstructionist' thought (if one risks this ridiculous designation which cannot but sound like its own parody), the term 'inhuman' has gained new weight, especially in the work of

Agamben and Badiou. The best way to approach it is via Freud's reluctance to endorse the injunction 'Love thy neighbour!' – the temptation to be resisted here is the ethical domestication of the neighbour – for example, what Emmanuel Levinas did with his notion of the neighbour as the abyssal point from which the call of ethical responsibility emanates. What Levinas thereby obfuscates is the monstrosity of the neighbour, a monstrosity on account of which Lacan applies to the neighbour the term Thing [*das Ding*], used by Freud to designate the ultimate object of our desires in its unbearable intensity and impenetrability. One should hear in this term all the connotations of horror fiction: the neighbour is the (Evil) Thing which potentially lurks beneath every homely human face. Just think about Stephen King's *Shining*, in which the father, a modest failed writer, gradually turns into a killing beast who, with an evil grin, goes on to slaughter his entire family. In a properly dialectical paradox, what Levinas, with all his celebration of Otherness, fails to take into account is not some underlying Sameness of all humans but the radically 'inhuman' Otherness itself: the Otherness of a human being reduced to inhumanity, the Otherness exemplified by the terrifying figure of the *Muselmann*, the 'living dead' in the concentration camps. At a different level, the same goes for Stalinist Communism. In the standard Stalinist narrative, even the concentration camps were a site of the fight against Fascism where imprisoned Communists were organizing networks of heroic resistance – in such a universe, of course, there is no place for the limit-experience of the *Muselmann*, of the living dead deprived of the capacity of human engagement – no wonder that Stalinist Communists were so eager to 'normalize' the camps into just another site of the anti-Fascist struggle, dismissing the *Muselmänner* as simply those who were to weak to endure the struggle.

It is against this background that one can understand why Lacan speaks of the *inhuman* core of the neighbour. Back in the 1960s, the era of structuralism, Louis Althusser launched the notorious formula of 'theoretical anti-humanism', allowing, demanding even, that it be supplemented by *practical humanism*. In our practice, we should act as humanists, respecting others, treating them as free persons with full dignity, creators of their world. However, in theory, we should no less always bear in mind that humanism is an ideology, the way we spontaneously experience our predicament, and that true knowledge of humans and their history should treat individuals not as autonomous subjects, but as elements in a structure which follows its own laws. In contrast to

Althusser, Lacan accomplishes the passage from theoretical to *practical anti-humanism*, i.e., to an ethics that goes beyond the dimension of what Nietzsche called 'human, all too human', and confronts the inhuman core of humanity. This does not mean only an ethics which no longer denies, but fearlessly takes into account, the latent monstrosity of being-human, the diabolic dimension which exploded in phenomena usually covered by the concept-name 'Auschwitz' – an ethics that would be still possible after Auschwitz, to paraphrase Adorno. This inhuman dimension is for Lacan, at the same time, the ultimate support of ethics.

In philosophical terms, this 'inhuman' dimension can be defined as that of a subject subtracted from all form of human 'individuality' or 'personality' (which is why, in today's popular culture, one of the exemplary figures of a pure subject is a non-human – alien, cyborg – who displays more fidelity to its task, and to dignity and freedom than its human counterparts, from the Schwarzenegger-figure in *Terminator* to the Rutger-Hauer-android in *Blade Runner*). Recall Husserl's dark dream, from his *Cartesian Meditations*, of how the transcendental cogito would remain unaffected by a plague that would annihilate all humanity: it is easy, apropos this example, to score cheap points about the self-destructive background of transcendental subjectivity, and about how Husserl misses the paradox of what Foucault, in his *Les mots et les choses*, called the 'transcendental-empirical doublet', of the link that forever attaches the transcendental ego to the empirical ego, so that the annihilation of the latter by definition leads to the disappearance of the first. However, what if, fully recognizing this dependence as a fact (and nothing more than this – a stupid fact of being), one nonetheless insists on the truth of its negation, the truth of the assertion of the independence of the subject with regard to the empirical individual *qua* living being? Is this independence not demonstrated in the ultimate gesture of risking one's life, on being ready to forsake one's being? It is against the background of this topic of the sovereign acceptance of death that one should reread the rhetorical turn often referred to as the proof of Robespierre's 'totalitarian' manipulation of his audience.[14] This turn took place during Robespierre's speech in the National Assembly on 11 Germinal Year II (31 March 1794); the previous night, Danton, Camille Desmoulins, and some others had been arrested, so many members of the Assembly were understandably afraid that their turn would also come. Robespierre directly indicates the moment is pivotal: 'Citizens, the moment has come to speak the truth.' He then goes on to evoke the fear floating in the room:

> One wants [*on veut*] to make you fear abuses of power, of the national power you have exercised. [. . .] One wants to make us fear that the people will fall victim to the Committees. [. . .] One fears that the prisoners are being oppressed [. . .][15]

The opposition is here between the impersonal 'one' (the instigators of fear are not personified) and the collective thus put under pressure, which almost imperceptibly shifts from the plural second-person 'you [*vous*]' to first-person 'us' (Robespierre gallantly includes himself into the collective). However, the final formulation introduces an ominous twist: it is no longer that 'one wants to make you/us fear', but that 'one fears', which means that the enemy stirring up fear is no longer outside 'you/us', members of the Assembly, it is here, among us, among 'you' addressed by Robespierre, corroding our unity from within. At this precise moment, Robespierre, in a true master stroke, assumes full subjectivization – waiting a little bit for the ominous effect of his words to take place, he then continues in the first-person *singular*: 'I say that anyone who trembles at this moment is guilty; for innocence never fears public scrutiny.'[16]

What can be more 'totalitarian' than this closed loop of 'your very fear of being guilty makes you guilty' – a weird superego-twisted version of the well-known motto 'the only thing to fear is fear itself'? One should nonetheless move beyond the quick dismissal of Robespierre's rhetorical strategy as the strategy of 'terrorist culpabilization', and to discern its moment of truth: there are no innocent bystanders in the crucial moments of revolutionary decision, because, in such moments, inno-cence itself – exempting oneself from the decision, going on as if the struggle I am witnessing does not really concern me – *is* the highest treason. That is to say, the fear of being accused of treason *is* my treason, because, even if I 'did not do anything against the revolution', this fear itself, the fact that it emerged in me, demonstrates that my subjective position is external to the revolution, that I experience 'revolution' as an external force threatening me.

But what goes on in this unique speech is even more revealing: Robespierre directly addresses the touchy question that has to arise in the mind of his public – how can he himself be sure that he will not be the next in line to be accused? He is not the master exempted from the collective, the 'I' outside 'we' – after all, he was once very close to Danton, a powerful figure now under arrest, so what if, tomorrow, his proximity to

Danton will be used against him? In short, how can Robespierre be sure that the process he has unleashed will not swallow him up? It is here that his position takes on a sublime greatness – he fully assumes the danger that now threatens Danton will tomorrow threaten him. The reason that he is so serene, that he is not afraid of this fate, is not that Danton was a traitor, while he, Robespierre, is pure, a direct embodiment of the people's Will; it is that he, Robespierre, *is not afraid to die* – his eventual death will be a mere accident which counts for nothing:

> What does danger matter to me? My life belongs to the homeland; my heart is free from fear; and if I were to die, I would do so without reproach and without ignominy.[17]

Consequently, insofar as the shift from 'we' to 'I' can effectively be determined as the moment when the democratic mask falls down and when Robespierre openly asserts himself as a Master (up to this point, we follow Lefort's analysis), the term Master has to be given here its full Hegelian weight: the Master is the figure of sovereignty, the one who is not afraid to die, who is ready to risk everything. In other words, the ultimate meaning of Robespierre's first-person singular ('I') is: I am not afraid to die. What authorizes him is just this, not any kind of direct access to the big Other; in other words, he does not claim that he has direct access to the people's Will which speaks through him. This is how Yamamoto Jocho, a Zen priest, described the proper attitude of a warrior:

> every day without fail one should consider oneself as dead. There is a saying of the elders that goes, 'Step from under the eaves and you're a dead man. Leave the gate and the enemy is waiting.' This is not a matter of being careful. It is to consider oneself as dead beforehand.[18]

This is why, according to Hillis Lory, many Japanese soldiers during World War II performed their own funerals before leaving for the battlefield:

> Many of the soldiers in the present war are so determined to die on the battlefield that they conduct their own public funerals before leaving for the front. This holds no element of the ridiculous to the Japanese. Rather, it is admired as the spirit of the true samurai who enters the battle with no thought of return.[19]

This pre-emptive self-exclusion from the domain of the living of course turns the soldier into a properly sublime figure. Instead of dismissing this feature as part of Fascist militarism, one should assert it as also constitutive of a radical revolutionary position: there is a straight line that runs from this acceptance of one's own disappearance to Mao Zedong's reaction to the atomic bomb threat from 1955:

> The United States cannot annihilate the Chinese nation with its small stack of atom bombs. Even if the US atom bombs were so powerful that, when dropped on China, they would make a hole right through the earth, or even blow it up, that would hardly mean anything to the universe as a whole, though it might be a major event for the solar system.[20]

There evidently is an 'inhuman madness' in this argument: is the fact that the destruction of the planet Earth 'would hardly mean anything to the universe as a whole' not a rather poor solace for the extinguished humanity? The argument only works if, in a Kantian way, one pre-supposes a pure transcendental subject unaffected by this catastrophe – a subject which, although non-existing in reality, *is* operative as a virtual point of reference. Every authentic revolutionary has to assume this attitude of thoroughly abstracting from, despising even, the imbecilic particularity of one's immediate existence, or, as Saint-Just formulated in an unsurpassable way this indifference towards what Benjamin called 'bare life': 'I despise the dust that forms me and speaks to you.'[21] Che Guevara approached the same line of thought when, in the midst of the unbearable tension of the Cuban missile crisis, he advocated a fearless approach of risking the new world war which would involve (at least) the total annihilation of the Cuban people – he praised the heroic readiness of the Cuban people to risk its own disappearance.

Another 'inhuman' dimension of the couple Virtue–Terror promoted by Robespierre is the rejection of habit (in the sense of the agency of realistic compromises). Every legal order (or every order of explicit normativity) has to rely on a complex 'reflexive' network of informal rules which tells us how are we to relate to the explicit norms, how are we to apply them: to what extent are we to take them literally, how and when are we allowed, solicited even, to disregard them, etc. – and this is the domain of habit. To know the habits of a society is *to know the meta-rules of how to apply its explicit norms*: when to use them or not use them;

when to violate them; when not to use a choice which is offered; when we are effectively obliged to do something, but have to pretend that we are doing it as a free choice (as in the case of potlatch). Recall the polite offer-meant-to-be-refused: it is a 'habit' to refuse such an offer, and anyone who accepts such an offer commits a vulgar blunder. The same goes for many political situations in which a choice is given *on condition that we make the right choice*: we are solemnly reminded that we can say no – but we are expected to reject this offer and enthusiastically say yes. With many sexual prohibitions, the situation is the opposite one: the explicit 'no' effectively functions as the implicit injunction 'do it, but in a discreet way!'. Measured against this background, revolutionary-egalitarian figures from Robespierre to John Brown are (potentially, at least) *figures without habits*: they refuse to take into account the habits that qualify the functioning of a universal rule:

> Such is the natural dominion of habit that we regard the most arbitrary conventions, sometimes indeed the most defective institutions, as absolute measures of truth or falsehood, justice or injustice. It does not even occur to us that most are inevitably still connected with the prejudices on which despotism fed us. We have been so long stooped under its yoke that we have some difficulty in raising ourselves to the eternal principles of reason; anything that refers to the sacred source of all law seems to us to take on an illegal character, and the very order of nature seems to us a disorder. The majestic movements of a great people, the sublime fervours of virtue often appear to our timid eyes as something like an erupting volcano or the overthrow of political society; and it is certainly not the least of the troubles bothering us, this contradiction between the weakness of our morals, the depravity of our minds, and the purity of principle and energy of character demanded by the free government to which we have dared aspire.[22]

To cast off the yoke of habit means: if all men are equal, then all men are to be effectively treated as equal; if blacks are also human, they should be immediately treated as such. Recall the early stages of the struggle against slavery in the US, which, even prior to the Civil War, culminated in armed conflict between the gradualism of compassionate liberals and the unique figure of John Brown:

African Americans were caricatures of people, they were characterized as buffoons and minstrels, they were the butt-end of jokes in American society. And even the abolitionists, as antislavery as they were, the majority of them did not see African Americans as equals. The majority of them, and this was something that African Americans complained about all the time, were willing to work for the end of slavery in the South but they were not willing to work to end discrimination in the North. [. . .] John Brown wasn't like that. For him, practicing egalitarianism was a first step toward ending slavery. And African Americans who came in contact with him knew this immediately. He made it very clear that he saw no difference, and he didn't make this clear by saying it, he made it clear by what he did.[23]

For this reason, John Brown is the *key* political figure in the history of the US: in his fervently Christian 'radical abolitionism', he came closest to introducing the Jacobin logic into the US political landscape:

John Brown considered himself a complete egalitarian. And it was very important for him to practice egalitarianism on every level. [. . .] He made it very clear that he saw no difference, and he didn't make this clear by saying it, he made it clear by what he did.[24]

Even today, long after the abolition of slavery, Brown is the dividing figure in American collective memory; those whites who support Brown are all the more precious – among them, surprisingly, Henry David Thoreau, the great opponent of violence: against the standard dismissal of Brown as blood-thirsty, foolish and insane, Thoreau[25] painted a portrait of a peerless man whose embrace of a cause was unparalleled; he even went so far as to liken Brown's execution (he states that he regards Brown as dead before his actual death) to Christ. Thoreau lashes out at the scores who voiced their displeasure and scorn for John Brown: the same people cannot understand Brown because of their concrete stances and 'dead' existences; they are truly not living, only a handful of men have lived.

It is, however, this very consistent egalitarianism which marks simultaneously the limitations of Jacobin politics. Recall Marx's fundamental insight about the 'bourgeois' limitation of the logic of equality: capitalist inequalities ('exploitations') are not the 'unprincipled violations of the principle of equality', but are absolutely inherent to the logic of equality, they are the paradoxical result of its consistent realization. What we have in mind here is not only the tired and old motif of how market exchange presupposes formally/legally equal subjects who meet and interact on the market; the crucial moment of Marx's critique of 'bourgeois' socialists is that capitalist exploitation does not involve any kind of 'unequal' exchange between the worker and the capitalist – this exchange is fully equal and 'just', ideally (in principle), the worker gets paid the full value of the commodity she is selling (her labour-power). Of course, radical bourgeois revolutionaries are aware of this limitation; however, the way they try to amend it is through a direct 'terrorist' imposition of more and more *de facto* equality (equal wages, equal health treatment . . .), which can only be imposed through new forms of formal inequality (different sorts of preferential treatments of the under-privileged). In short, the axiom of 'equality' means either not enough (it remains the abstract form of actual inequality) or too much (enforcing 'terrorist' equality) – it is a formalist notion in a strict dialectical sense, i.e., its limitation is precisely that its form is not concrete enough, but a mere neutral container of some content that eludes this form.

The problem here is not terror as such – our task today is precisely to reinvent emancipatory terror. The problem lies elsewhere: egalitarian political 'extremism' or 'excessive radicalism' should always be read as a phenomenon of ideologico-political *displacement*: as an index of its opposite, of a limitation, of a refusal effectively to 'go all the way'. What was the Jacobins' recourse to radical 'terror' if not a kind of hysterical acting out bearing witness to their inability to disturb the very fundamentals of economic order (private property, etc.)? And does the same not go even for the so-called 'excesses' of Political Correctness? Do they also not display the retreat from disturbing the effective (economic etc.) causes of racism and sexism? Perhaps, then, the time has come to render problematic the standard topos, shared by practically all the 'postmodern' Leftists, according to which political 'totalitarianism' some-how results from the predominance of material production and tech-nology over intersubjective communication and/or symbolic practice, as if the root of the political terror resides in the fact that the 'principle' of instrumental reason, of the technological exploitation of nature, is extended also to society, so that people are treated as raw material to be transformed into a New Man. What if it is the exact *opposite* which holds? What if political 'terror' signals precisely that the sphere of (material) production is *denied* its autonomy and *subordinated* to political logic? Is it not that all forms of political 'terror', from the Jacobins to the Maoist Cultural Revolution, presuppose the foreclosure of the sphere of production proper, its reduction to the terrain of political battle? In other words, what it effectively amounts to is nothing less than the abandonment of Marx's key insight that the political struggle is a spectacle which, in order to be deciphered, has to be referred to the sphere of economics ('if Marxism had any analytical value for *political* theory, was it not in the insistence that the problem of freedom was contained in the social relations implicitly declared "unpolitical" – that is, naturalized – in liberal discourse'[26]).

As to philosophical roots of this limitation of egalitarian terror, it is relatively easy to discern the roots of what went wrong with Jacobin terror as lying in Rousseau who was ready to pursue to its 'Stalinist' extreme the paradox of the general will:

> Apart from this original contract, the votes of the greatest number always bind the rest; and this is a consequence of the contract itself. Yet it may be asked how a man can be at once free and forced to conform to wills which are not his own. How can the opposing minority be both free and subject to laws to which they have not consented? I answer that the question is badly formulated. The citizen consents to all the laws, even to those that are passed against his will, and even to those which punish him when he dares to break any one of them. The constant will of all the members of the state is the general will; it is through it that they are citizens and free. When a law is proposed in the people's assembly, what is asked of them is not precisely whether they approve of the proposition or reject it, but whether it is in conformity with the general will which is theirs; each by giving his vote gives his opinion on this question, and the counting of votes yields a declaration of the general will. When, therefore, the opinion contrary to my own prevails, this proves only that I have made a mistake, and that what I believed to be the general will was not so. If my particular opinion had prevailed against the general will, I should have done something other than what I had willed, and then I should not have been free.[27]

The 'totalitarian' catch here is the short-circuit between the constative and the performative: by reading the voting procedure not as a performative act of decision, but as a constative one, as the act of expressing the opinion on (of guessing) what the general will is (which is thus substantialized into something that *pre-exists* voting), he avoids the deadlock of the rights of those who remain in the minority (they should obey the decision of the majority, because in the result of voting, they learn what the general will really is). In other words, those who remain in the minority are not simply a minority: in learning the result of the vote (which runs against their individual votes), they do not simply learn that they are a minority – what they learn is that they were *mistaken* about the nature of the general will.

The parallel between this substantialization of the general will and the religious notion of Predestination cannot but strike the eye: in the case of Predestination, fate is also substantialized into a decision that precedes the process, so that what is at stake in individuals' activities is not to performatively constitute their fate, but to discover (or guess) their pre-existing fate. What is obfuscated in both cases is the dialectical reversal of contingency into necessity, i.e., the way the outcome of a contingent process is the appearance of necessity: things retroactively 'will have been' necessary. This reversal was described by Jean-Pierre Dupuy:

> The catastrophic event is inscribed into the future as a destiny, for sure, but also as a contingent accident: it could not have taken place, even if, in *futur antérieur*, it appears as necessary. [. . .] If an outstanding event takes place, a catastrophe, for example, it could not not have taken place; nonetheless, insofar as it did not take place, it is not inevitable. It is thus the event's actualization – the fact that it takes place – which retroactively creates its necessity.[28]

Dupuy provides the example of the French presidential elections in May 1995; here is the January forecast of the main polling institute: 'If, on next May 8, M. Balladur is elected, one can say that the presidential election was decided before it even took place.' If – accidentally – an event takes place, it creates the preceding chain which makes it appear inevitable: *this*, not the commonplaces on how the underlying necessity expresses itself in and through the accidental play of appearances, is *in nuce* the Hegelian dialectics of contingency and necessity. The same goes for the October Revolution (once the Bolsheviks won and stabilized their hold on power, their victory appeared as an outcome and expression of a deeper historical necessity), and even of Bush's much contested first US presidential victory (after the contingent and contested Florida majority, his victory retroactively appears as an expression of a deeper US political trend). In this sense, although we are determined by destiny, we are nonetheless *free to choose our destiny*. This, according to Dupuy, is also how we should approach the ecological crisis: not to 'realistically' appraise the possibilities of the catastrophe, but to accept it as Destiny in the precise Hegelian sense: like the election of Balladur, 'if the catastrophe happens, one can say that its occurrence was decided before it even took place.' Destiny and free action (to block the 'if') thus go hand in hand: freedom is its most radical the freedom to change one's Destiny.[29] Which brings us back to our central question: what would a Jacobin politics which took into account this retroactive-contingent rise of universality look like? How are we to reinvent the Jacobin terror?

Let us return to Merleau-Ponty's *Humanism and Terror*: according to its argument, even some Stalinists themselves, when (in half-private, usually) forced to admit that many of the victims of the purges were innocent, and were accused and killed because 'the Party needed their blood to fortify its unity', imagine the future moment of final victory when all the necessary victims will be given their due, and their innocence and their highest sacrifice for the Cause will be recognized. This is what Lacan, in his seminar on *The Ethics of Psychoanalysis*,[30] refers to as the 'perspective of the Last Judgement', a perspective even more clearly discernible in one of the key terms of Stalinist discourse, that of the 'objective guilt' and 'objective meaning' of your acts: while you can be an honest individual who acted with most sincere intentions, you are nonetheless 'objectively guilty,' if your acts serve reactionary forces – and it is, of course, the Party which has the direct access to what your acts 'objectively mean'. Here, again, we not only get the perspective of the Last Judgement (which formulates the 'objective meaning' of your acts), but also the present agent who already has the unique ability to judge today's events and acts from this perspective.[31.]

We can see now why Lacan's motto 'il n'y a pas de grand Autre [there is no big Other]' brings us to the very core of the ethical problematic: what it excludes is precisely this 'perspective of the Last Judgement', the idea that somewhere – even if as a thoroughly virtual point of reference, even if we concede that we cannot ever occupy its place and pass the actual judgement – there must be a standard which allows us to take the measure of our acts and pronounce their 'true meaning', their true ethical status. Even Jacques Derrida's notion of 'deconstruction as justice' seems to rely on a utopian hope which sustains the spectre of 'infinite justice', forever postponed, always to come, but nonetheless here as the ultimate horizon of our activity. Lacan himself pointed the way out of this deadlock by referring to Kant's philosophy as the crucial antecedent of psychoanalytical ethics. As such, Kantian ethics effectively harbours a 'terrorist' potential – a feature which points in this direction would be Kant's well-known thesis that Reason without Intuition is empty, while Intuition without Reason is blind: is not its political counterpart Robespierre's dictum according to which Virtue without Terror is impotent, while Terror without Virtue is lethal, striking blindly?

According to the standard critique, the limitation of the Kantian universalist ethic of the 'categorical imperative' (the unconditional injunction to do our duty) resides in its formal indeterminacy: moral Law does not tell me *what* my duty is, it merely tells me *that* I should accomplish my duty, and so leaves the space open for empty voluntarism (whatever I decide to be my duty *is* my duty). However, far from being a limitation, this very feature brings us to the core of Kantian ethical autonomy: it is not possible to derive the concrete norms I have to follow in my specific situation from the moral Law itself – which means that the subject herself has to assume the responsibility of translating the abstract injunction of the moral Law into a series of concrete obligations. The full acceptance of this paradox compels us to reject any reference to duty as an excuse: 'I know this is heavy and can be painful, but what can I do, this is my duty . . .' Kant's ethics of unconditional duty is often taken as justifying such an attitude – no wonder Adolf Eichmann himself referred to Kantian ethics when he tried to justify his role in planning and executing the Holocaust: he was just doing his duty and obeying the *Führer*'s orders. However, the aim of Kant's emphasis on the subject's full moral autonomy and responsibility is precisely to prevent any such manoeuvre of displacing the blame onto some figure of the big Other.

The standard motto of ethical rigour is: 'There is no excuse for not accomplishing one's duty!' Although Kant's well-known maxim *Du kannst, denn du sollst!* ('You can, because you must!') seems to offer a new version of this motto, he implicitly complements it with its much more uncanny inversion: 'There is no excuse for accomplishing one's duty!' The very reference to duty as the excuse to do my duty should be rejected as hypocritical. Recall the proverbial example of a severe and sadistic teacher who subjects his pupils to merciless discipline and torture;

his excuse to himself (and to others) is: 'I myself find it hard to exert such pressure on the poor kids, but what can I do – it's my duty!' This is what psychoanalytical ethics thoroughly forbids: in it, I am fully responsible not only for doing my duty, but no less for determining what my duty is.

Along the same lines, in his writings of 1917, Lenin saves his utmost acerbic irony for those who engage in the endless search for some kind of 'guarantee' for the revolution; this guarantee assumes two main forms: either the reified notion of social Necessity (one should not risk the revolution too early; one has to wait for the right moment, when the situation is 'mature' with regard to the laws of historical development: 'it is too early for the socialist revolution, the working class is not yet mature') or the normative ('democratic') legitimacy ('the majority of the population is not on our side, so the revolution would not really be democratic') – as Lenin repeatedly puts, it is as if, before the revolutionary agent risks the seizure of the state power, it should get permission from some figure of the big Other (organize a referendum which will ascertain that the majority supports the revolution). With Lenin, as with Lacan, the revolution *ne s'autorise que d'elle-même*: one should assume the revolutionary *act* not covered by the big Other – the fear of taking power 'prematurely', the search for a guarantee, is the fear of the abyss of the act.

It is only such a radical stance that allows us to break with today's predominant mode of politics, post-political biopolitics, which is a politics of fear, formulated as a defence against a potential victimization or harassment. Therein resides the true line of separation between radical emancipatory politics and the politics of the status quo: it is not the difference between two different positive visions, sets of axioms, but, rather, the difference between the politics based on a set of universal axioms and the politics which renounces the very constitutive dimension of the political, since it resorts to fear as its ultimate mobilizing principle: fear of immigrants, fear of crime, fear of godless sexual depravity, fear of the excessive state itself (with its burdensome taxation), fear of ecological catastrophes – such a (post)politics always amounts to a frightening rallying of frightened men. This is why the big event – not only in Europe – in early 2006 was that anti-immigration politics 'went mainstream': the umbilical link that connected them to far Right fringe parties was finally cut. From France to Germany, from Austria to Holland, in the new spirit of pride in one's cultural and historical identity, the main parties now find it acceptable to stress that the immigrants are guests who have to accommodate themselves to the cultural values that define the host society − it is 'our country, love it or leave it'.

How are we to break out of this (post)politics of fear? The biopolitical administration of life is the true content of global liberal democracy, and this introduces the tension between democratic form and administrative-regulatory content. What, then, would be the opposite of biopolitics? What if we take the risk of resuscitating the good old 'dictatorship of the proletariat' as the only way to break biopolitics? This cannot but sound ridiculous today, it cannot but appear that these are two incompatible terms from different fields, with no shared space: the latest political power analysis versus the old discredited Communist mythology . . . And yet: this is the only true choice today. The term 'proletarian dictatorship' continues to point towards the key problem.

A commonsense reproach arises here: why dictatorship? Why not true democracy or simply the power of the proletariat? 'Dictatorship' does not mean the opposite of democracy, but democracy's own underlying mode of functioning − from the very beginning, the thesis on the 'dictatorship of the proletariat' involved the presupposition that it was the opposite of other form(s) of dictatorship, since the entire field of state power is that of dictatorship. When Lenin designated liberal democracy as a form of bourgeois dictatorship, he did not imply a simplistic notion about how democracy is really manipulated, a mere façade, or how some secret clique is really in power and controls things, and that, if threatened with losing power in democratic elections, it would show its true face and assume direct control. What he meant is that the very *form* of the bourgeois-democratic state, the sovereignty of its power in its ideologico-political presuppositions, embodies a 'bourgeois' logic.

One should thus use the term 'dictatorship' in the precise sense in which democracy also is a form of dictatorship, i.e., as a purely *formal* determination. Many like to point out how self-questioning is consti-tutive of democracy, how democracy always allows, solicits us even, to question its own features. However, this self-referentiality has to stop at some point: even the 'free-est' elections cannot put into question the legal procedures that legitimize and organize them, the state apparatuses that guarantee (by force, if necessary) the electoral process, and so on. The state in its institutional aspect is a massive presence which cannot be accounted for in the terms of the representation of interests − the democratic illusion is that it can. Badiou conceptualizes this excess as the excess of the state's re-presentation over what it represents; one can also put it in Benjaminian terms: while democracy can more or less eliminate constituted violence, it still has to rely continuously on the constitutive violence.

Recall the lesson of Hegelian 'concrete universality' – imagine a philosophical debate between a hermeneutician, a deconstructionist and an analytic philosopher. What they sooner or later discover is that they do not simply occupy positions within a shared common space called 'philosophy': what distinguishes them is the very notion of what philosophy as such is; in other words, an analytic philosopher perceives the global field of philosophy and the respective differences between the participants in a different manner from a hermeneutician: what is different between them is differences themselves, which are what render their true differences in a first approach invisible – the gradual classificatory logic of 'this is what we share, and here our differences begin' breaks down. For today's cognitivist analytic philosopher, after the cognitivist turn, philosophy has finally reached the maturity of serious reasoning, leaving behind metaphysical speculations. For a hermeneutician, analytic philosophy is, on the contrary, the end of philosophy, the final loss of a true philosophical stance, the transformation of philosophy into another positive science. So when the participants in the debate get struck by this more fundamental gap that separates them, they stumble upon the moment of 'dictatorship'. And, in a homologous way, the same goes for political democracy: its dictatorial dimension becomes palpable when the struggle turns into the struggle about the field of struggle itself.

So what about the proletariat? Insofar as the proletariat is, within a social edifice, its 'out of joint' part, the element which, while a formal part of this edifice, has no determinate place within it, the 'part of no-part' which stands for universality, the 'dictatorship of the proletariat' means: the direct empowerment of universality, so that those who are the 'part of no-part' determine the tone. They are egalitarian-universalist for purely formal reasons: as the part of no-part, they lack the particular features that would legitimate their place within the social body – they belong to the set of society without belonging to any of its sub-sets; as such, their belonging is directly universal. Here, the logic of the representation of multiple particular interests and their mediation through compromises reaches its limit; every dictatorship breaks with this logic of representation (which is why the simplistic definition of Fascism as the dictatorship of finance capital is wrong: Marx already knew that Napoleon III, this proto-Fascist, broke with the logic of representation). One should thus thoroughly demystify the scarecrow of the 'dictatorship of the proletariat': at its most basic, it stands for the tremulous moment when the complex web of representations is suspended due to the direct intrusion of universality into the political field. With regard to the French Revolution, it was, significantly, Danton, *not* Robespierre, who provided the most concise formula of the imperceptible shift from 'dictatorship of the proletariat' to statist violence, or, in Benjamin's terms, from divine to mythic violence: 'Let us be terrible so that the people will not have to be.'[32] For Danton, Jacobin revolutionary state terror was a kind of pre-emptive action whose true aim was not to seek revenge against the enemies but to prevent the direct 'divine' violence of the *sans-culottes*, of the people themselves. In other words, let us do what the people demand us to do *so that they will not do it themselves* . . .

From Ancient Greece, we have a name for this intrusion: democracy. That is to say, what is democracy, at its most elementary? A phenomenon which, for the first time, appeared in Ancient Greece when the members of *demos* (those with no firmly determined place in the hierarchical social edifice) not only demanded that their voice be heard against those in power. They not only protested against the wrongs they suffered and wanted their voice to be recognized and included in the public sphere, on an equal footing with the ruling oligarchy and aristocracy; even more, they, the excluded, those with no fixed place within the social edifice, presented themselves as the embodiment of the Whole of Society, of the true Universality: 'we – the "nothing", not counted in the order – are the people, we are All against others who stand only for their particular privileged interest.' The political conflict proper designates the tension between the structured social body in which each part has its place, and 'the part with no-part' which unsettles this order on account of the empty principle of universality, of what Etienne Balibar calls *égaliberté*, the principled equality of all men *qua* speaking beings – up to and including the *liumang*, 'hoodlums', in today's China, those who are displaced and float freely, without work or lodging, but also without cultural or sexual identities and without official papers.

This identification of the part of society with no properly defined place within it (or resisting the allocated subordinated place within it) with the Whole is the elementary gesture of politicization, discernible in all great democratic events from the French Revolution (in which *le tiers état* proclaimed itself identical to the Nation as such, against the aristocracy and clergy) to the demise of the East European socialism (in which dissident 'fora' proclaimed themselves representative of the entire society against the Party *nomenklatura*). In this precise sense, politics and democracy are synonymous: the basic aim of antidemocratic politics always and by definition is and was depoliticization, the demand that 'things should return to normal', with each individual sticking to her particular job. And this brings us to the inevitable paradoxical conclusion: *the 'dictatorship of the proletariat' is another name for the violence of the democratic explosion itself.* The 'dictatorship of the proletariat' is thus the zero-level at which the difference between legitimate and illegitimate state power is suspended, i.e., at which the state power *as such* is illegitimate. Saint-Just said in November 1792: 'Every king is a rebel and a usurper.' This phrase is a cornerstone of emancipatory politics: there is no 'legitimate' king as opposed to the usurper, since *being a king is in itself a usurpation*, in the same sense that, for Proudhon, property as such is theft. What we have here is the Hegelian 'negation of the negation', the passage from the simple-direct negation ('this king is not a legitimate one, he is a usurper'), to the inherent self-negation (an 'authentic king' is an oxymoron, being a king *is* usurpation). This is why, for Robespierre, the trial of the king is not a trial at all:

> There is no trial to be held here. Louis is not a defendant. You are not judges. You are not, you cannot be anything but statesmen and representatives of the nation. You have no sentence to pronounce for or against a man, but a measure of public salvation to implement, an act of national providence to perform. [. . .] Louis was king, and the Republic is founded: the famous question you are considering is settled by those words alone. Louis was dethroned by his crimes; Louis denounced the French people as rebellious; to chastise it, he called on the arms of his fellow tyrants; victory and the people decided that he was the rebellious one: therefore Louis cannot be judged; either he is already condemned or the Republic is not acquitted. Proposing to put Louis on trial, in whatever way that could be done, would be to regress towards royal and constitutional despotism; it is a counter-revolutionary idea, for it means putting the revolution itself in contention. In fact, if Louis can still be put on trial, then he can be acquitted; he may be innocent; what am I saying! He is presumed to be so until he has been tried. But if Louis is acquitted, if Louis can be presumed innocent, what becomes of the revolution?[33]

This strange coupling of democracy and dictatorship is grounded in the tension that pertains to the very notion of democracy. What Chantal Mouffe calls the 'democratic paradox' almost symmetrically inverts the fundamental paradox of authoritarian Fascism: if the wager of (institutionalized) democracy is to integrate the antagonistic struggle itself into the institutional/differential space, transforming it into regulated agonism, Fascism proceeds in the opposite direction. While Fascism, in its mode of activity, brings the antagonistic logic to its extreme (talking about the 'struggle to death' between itself and its enemies, and always maintaining – if not realizing – a minimal extra-institutional threat of violence, the 'direct pressure of the people' by-passing the complex legal-institutional channels), it posits as its political goal precisely the opposite, an extremely ordered hierarchical social body (no wonder Fascism always relies on organicist-corporatist metaphors). This contrast can be nicely rendered in the terms of the Lacanian opposition between the 'subject of enunciation' and the 'subject of the enunciated (content)': while democracy admits antagonistic struggle as its goal (in Lacanese: as its enunciated, its content), its procedure is regulated-systemic; Fascism, on the contrary, tries to impose the goal of hierarchically structured harmony through the means of an unbridled antagonism.

In a homologous way, the ambiguity of the petty bourgeoisie, this contradiction embodied (as already Marx put it apropos Proudhon), is best exemplified by the way it relates to politics: on the one hand, the middle class is against politicization – it just wants to sustain its way of life, to be left to work and lead its life in peace (which is why it tends to support the authoritarian coups which promise to put an end to the crazy political mobilization of society, so that everybody can return to his or her proper place). On the other hand, the petty bourgeois – in the guise of the threatened patriotic hard-working moral majority – are the main instigators of the grass-roots mass mobilization (in the guise of Rightist populism – say, in France today, where the only force truly disturbing post-political technocratic-humanitarian administration is Le Pen's National Front).

There are two elementary and irreducible sides to democracy: the violent egalitarian imposition of those who are 'surnumerary', the 'part of no-part', those who, while formally included within the social edifice, have no determinate place within it; and the regulated (more or less) universal procedure of choosing those who will exert power. How do these two sides relate to each other? What if democracy in the second sense (the regulated procedure of registering the 'people's voice') is ultimately *a defence against itself*, against democracy in the sense of the violent intrusion of the egalitarian logic that disturbs the hierarchical functioning of the social edifice, an attempt to re-functionalize this excess, to make it a part of the normal running of the social system?

The problem is thus: how to regulate/institutionalize the very violent egalitarian democratic impulse, how to prevent it from being drowned in democracy in the second sense of the term (regulated procedure)? If there is no way to do it, then 'authentic' democracy remains a momentary utopian outburst which, the proverbial morning after, has to be normalized.[34]

The Orwellian proposition 'democracy is terror' is thus democracy's 'infinite judgement', its highest speculative identity. This dimension gets lost in Claude Lefort's notion of democracy as involving the empty place of power, the constitutive gap between the place of power and the contingent agents who, for a limited period, can occupy that place. Paradoxically, the underlying premise of democracy is thus not only that there is no political agent which has a 'natural' right to power, but, much more radically, that the 'people' itself, the ultimate source of sovereign power in democracy, does not exist as a substantial entity. In the Kantian perspective, the democratic notion of the 'people' is a negative concept, a concept whose function is merely to designate a certain limit: it prohibits any determinate agent from ruling with total sovereignty. (The only moments when the 'people exists' are the democratic elections, which are precisely the moments of the disintegration of the entire social edifice – in elections, the 'people' is reduced to a mechanical collection of individuals.) The claim that the people *does* exist is the basic axiom of 'totalitarianism', and the mistake of 'totalitarianism' is strictly homologous to the Kantian misuse ('paralogism') of political reason: 'the People exists' through a determinate political agent which acts as if it directly embodies (not only re-presents) the People, its true Will (the totalitarian Party and its Leader), i.e., in the terms of transcendental critique, as a direct phenomenal embodiment of the noumenal People . . . The obvious link between this notion of democracy and Lacan's notion of the inconsistency of the big Other was elaborated by Jacques-Alain Miller, among others:

> Is 'democracy' a master-signifier? Without any doubt. It is the master-signifier which says that there is no master-signifier, at least not a master-signifier which would stand alone, that every master-signifier has to insert itself wisely among others. Democracy is Lacan's big S of

the barred A, which says: I am the signifier of the fact that Other has a hole, or that it doesn't exist.[35]

Of course, Miller is aware that *every* master-signifier bears witness to the fact that there is no master-signifier, no Other of the Other, that there is a lack in the Other, etc. – the very gap between S1 and S2 occurs because of this lack (as with God in Spinoza, the Master-Signifier by definition fills in the gap in the series of 'ordinary' signifiers). The difference is that, with democracy, this lack is directly inscribed into the social system, it is institutionalized in a set of procedures and regulations – no wonder, then, that Miller approvingly quotes Marcel Gauchet regarding how, in democracy, truth only offers itself 'in division and decomposition' (and one cannot but note with irony how Stalin and Mao made the same claim, although with a 'totalitarian' twist: in politics, truth only emerges through the ruthless divisions of class struggle . . .).

It is easy to note how, from within this Kantian horizon of democracy, the 'terrorist' aspect of democracy – the violent egalitarian imposition of those who are 'surnumerary', the 'part of no-part' – can only appear as its 'totalitarian' distortion, i.e., how, within this horizon, the line that separates the authentic democratic explosion of revolutionary terror from the 'totalitarian' Party-State regime (or, to put it in reactionary terms, the line that separates the 'mob rule of the dispossessed' from the Party-State's brutal oppression of the 'mob') is obliterated. (One can, of course, argue that direct 'mob rule' is inherently unstable and that it turns necessarily into its opposite, a tyranny over the mob itself; however, this shift in no way changes the fact that, precisely, we are dealing with a shift, a radical turnaround.) Foucault deals with this shift in his writings on the Iranian Revolution, where he opposes the historical reality of a complex process of social, cultural, economic, political, and other transformations to the magic event of the revolt which somehow suspends the web of historical causality – it is irreducible to it:

> The man in revolt is ultimately inexplicable. There must be an uprooting that interrupts the unfolding of history, and its long series of reasons why, for a man 'really' to prefer the risk of death over the certainty of having to obey.[36]

One should be aware of the Kantian connotation of these propositions: a revolt is an act of freedom which momentarily suspends the nexus of historical causality, in other words in revolt, the noumenal dimension transpires. The paradox, of course, is that this noumenal dimension coincides with its opposite, with the pure surface of a phenomenon: the noumenon not only appears, the noumenal is what is, in a phenomenon, irreducible to the causal network of reality that generated this phenomenon – in short, the *noumenon is phenomenon qua phenomenon*. There is a clear link between this irreducible character of the phenomenon and Deleuze's notion of event as the flux of becoming, as a surface emergence that cannot be reduced to its 'bodily' causes. His reply to the conservative critics who denounce the miserable and even terrifying actual results of a revolutionary upheaval is that they remain blind to the dimension of becoming:

> It is fashionable these days to condemn the horrors of revolution. It's nothing new; English Romanticism is permeated by reflections on Cromwell very similar to present-day reflections on Stalin. They say revolutions turn out badly. But they're constantly confusing two different things, the way revolutions turn out historically and people's revolutionary becoming. These relate to two different sets of people. Men's only hope lies in a revolutionary becoming: the only way of casting off their shame or responding to what is intolerable.[37]

Deleuze refers here to revolutionary explosions in a way which is strictly parallel to Foucault:

> The Iranian movement did not experience the 'law' of revolutions that would, some say, make the tyranny that already secretly inhabited them reappear underneath the blind enthusiasm of the masses. What constituted the most internal and the most intensely lived part of the uprising touched, in an unmediated fashion, on an already over-crowded political chessboard, but such contact is not identity. The spirituality of those who were going to their deaths has no similarity whatsoever with the bloody government of a fundamentalist clergy. The Iranian clerics want to authenticate their regime through the significations that the uprising had. It is no different to discredit the fact of the uprising on the grounds that there is today a government of mullahs. In both cases, there is 'fear', fear of what just happened last fall in Iran, something of which the world had not seen an example for a long time.[38]

Foucault is here effectively Deleuzian: what interests him are not the Iranian events at the level of actual social reality and its causal interactions, but the evental surface, the pure virtuality of the 'spark of life' which only accounts for the uniqueness of the Event. What took place in Iran in the interstices of two epochs of social reality was not the explosion of the People as a substantial entity with a set of properties, but the event of becoming-People. The point is thus not the shift in relations of power and domination between actual socio-political agents, the redistribution of social control, etc., but the very fact of transcending – or, rather, momentarily cancelling – this very domain, of the emergence of a totally different domain of 'collective will' as a pure Sense-Event in which all differences are obliterated, rendered irrelevant. Such an event is not only new with regard to what was going on before, it is new 'in itself' and thus forever remains new.

It is against this background that one can formulate a critique of Jacques Rancière's political aesthetics, of his idea of the aesthetic dimension of the political act proper: a democratic explosion reconfigures the established hierarchical 'police' order of social space; it stages a spectacle of a different order, of a different *partage* of the public space.[39] In today's 'society of spectacle', such an aesthetic reconfiguration has lost its subversive dimension: it can all too easily be appropriated by the existing order. The true task does not lie in momentary democratic explosions which undermine the established 'police' order, but in the dimension designated by Badiou as that of the 'fidelity' to the Event: how to translate/inscribe the democratic explosion into the positive 'police' order, how to impose on social reality a *new* lasting order. *This* is the properly 'terrorist' dimension of every authentic democratic explosion: the brutal imposition of a new order. And this is why, while everybody loves democratic rebellions, the spectacular/carnivalesque explosions of the popular will, anxiety arises when this will wants to persist, to institutionalize itself – and the more 'authentic' the rebellion is, the more 'terrorist' is this institutionalization. It is at this level that one should search for the decisive moment of a revolutionary process: say, in the case of the October Revolution, not the explosion of 1917-18, not even the civil war that followed, but the intense experimentations of the early 1920s, the (desperate, often ridiculous) attempts to invent new rituals of daily life: with what to replace the pre-revolutionary procedures of marriage and funerals? How to organize the most common interaction in a factory, in an apartment block? It is at this level of what, as opposed to the 'abstract terror' of the 'big' political revolution, one is tempted to call the 'concrete terror' of imposing a new order onto daily life, that the Jacobins and both the Soviet revolution and the Chinese revolution ultimately failed – not for the lack of attempts in this direction, for sure. The Jacobins were at their best not in the theatrics of Terror, but in the utopian explosions of political imagination apropos the reorganization of daily life: everything was there, proposed in the course of the frantic activity condensed in a couple of years, from the self-organization of women to the communal homes in which the old would be able to spend their last years in peace and dignity. (So what about Robespierre's rather ridiculous attempt to impose a new civic religion celebrating a Supreme Being? Robespierre himself formulated succinctly the main reason for his opposition to atheism: 'Atheism is aristocratic.'[40] Atheism was for him the ideology of the cynical-hedonistic aristocrats who had lost all sense of historical mission.)

The harsh consequence to be accepted here is that this excess of egalitarian democracy over the democratic procedure can only 'institutionalize' itself in the guise of its opposite, as revolutionary-democratic *terror*. So, again, how to reinvent this terror for today? In his *Logiques des mondes*, Alain Badiou[41] elaborates the eternal Idea of the politics of revolutionary justice at work from the ancient Chinese 'legists' through the Jacobins to Lenin and Mao – it consists of four moments: *voluntarism* (the belief that one can 'move mountains', ignoring 'objective' laws and obstacles), *terror* (a ruthless will to crush the enemy of the people), *egalitarian justice* (its immediate brutal imposition, with no understanding for the 'complex circumstances' which allegedly compel us to proceed gradually), and, last but not least, *trust in the people* – suffice it to recall two examples here, Robespierre himself, his 'great truth' ('the characteristic of popular government is to be trustful towards the people and severe towards itself'), and Mao's critique of Stalin's *Economic Problems of Socialism in the USSR*, where he qualifies Stalin's point of view as 'almost altogether wrong. The basic error is mistrust of the peasants.').[42] And is the only appropriate way to counter the threat of ecological catastrophe that looms over our horizon not precisely the combination of these four moments? What is demanded is:

– strict *egalitarian justice* (all people should pay the same price in terms of renunciations, i.e., one should impose the same world-wide norms of per capita energy consumption, carbon dioxide emissions, etc.; the developed nations should not be allowed to poison the environment at the present rate, blaming the developing Third World countries, from Brazil to China, for ruining our shared environment with their rapid development);

– *terror* (ruthless punishment of all who violate the imposed protective measures, inclusive of severe limitations of liberal 'freedoms', technological control of the prospective law-breakers);

– *voluntarism* (the only way to confront the threat of the ecological catastrophe is by means of large-scale collective decisions which will run counter to the 'spontaneous' immanent logic of capitalist development – it is not a question of helping the historical tendency or necessity to realize itself, but to 'stop the train' of history which runs towards the precipice of global catastrophe;

– and, last but not least, all this combined with the *trust in the people* (the wager that the large majority of the people support these severe measures, see them as their own, and are ready to participate in their enforcement). One should not be afraid to assert, as a combination of terror and trust in the people, the reactivation of one of the figures of all egalitarian-revolutionary terror, the 'informer' who denounces the culprits to the authorities. (Already in the case of the Enron scandal, *Time* magazine was right to celebrate the insiders who tipped off the financial authorities as true public heroes.)[43]

Back in the early seventeenth century, after the establishment of the shogun regime, Japan made a unique collective decision to isolate itself from foreign cultures and to pursue its own path of a contained life of balanced reproduction, focused on cultural refinement, avoiding wild expansion. Was the ensuing period which lasted till the middle of the nineteenth century really just an isolationist dream from which Japan was cruelly awakened by Commodore Perry on the American warship? What if the dream is that we can go on indefinitely in our expansionism? What if we all need to repeat, *mutatis mutandis*, the Japanese decision, and collectively decide to intervene into our pseudo-natural development, to change its direction? The tragedy is that the very idea of such a collective decision is discredited today. Apropos of the disintegration of state socialism two decades ago, one should not forget that, at approximately the same time, the Western social-democratic welfare state ideology was also dealt a crucial blow; it also ceased to function as the imaginary able to arouse a collective passionate following. The notion that 'the time of the welfare state has passed' is today a piece of commonly accepted wisdom. What these two defeated ideologies shared is the notion that humanity as a collective subject has the capacity to somehow limit impersonal and anonymous socio-historical development, to steer it in a desired direction.

Today, such a notion is quickly dismissed as 'ideological' and/or 'totalitarian': the social process is again perceived as dominated by an anonymous Fate beyond social control. The rise of global capitalism is presented to us as such a Fate, against which one cannot fight – one either adapts oneself to it, or one falls out of step with history and one is crushed. The only thing one can do is to make global capitalism as humane as possible, to fight for 'global capitalism with a human face' (this is what, ultimately, the Third Way is – or, rather, *used to be* – about). The sound barrier will have to be broken here, the risk will have to be taken to endorse again large-scale collective decisions – this, perhaps, is the main legacy of Robespierre and his comrades to us today.

Moments before Robespierre's death, the executioner noticed that his head would not fit into the guillotine with the bandages applied to his jaw wounds, so he brutally ripped them off; from Robespierre's ruined throat emerged a ghastly piercing scream, only cut short as the blade fell upon his neck. The status of this last scream is legendary: it gave rise to a whole panoply of interpretations, mostly along the lines of the terrifying inhuman screech of the parasitical evil spirit which signals its impotent protest when it is losing possession of its host human body – as if, at this final moment, Robespierre humanized himself, discarding the persona of revolutionary virtue embodied and emerging as a miserable scared human being.

The popular image of Robespierre is that of a kind of Elephant Man inverted: while the latter had a terribly deformed body hiding a gentle and intelligent soul, Robespierre was a kind and polite person hiding ice-cold cruel determination signalled by his green eyes. As such, Robespierre serves perfectly today's anti-totalitarian liberals who no longer need to portray him as a cruel monster with a sneering evil smile, as was the case for nineteenth-century reactionaries: everyone is ready to recognize his moral integrity and full devotion to the revolutionary cause, since his very purity is the problem, the cause of all trouble, as is signalled by the title of the latest biography of Robespierre, Ruth Scurr's *Fatal Purity*.[44] The titles of some of the reviews of the book are indicative: 'Terror Wears a Sea-Green Coat', 'The Good Terrorist', 'Virtue's Demon Executioner', and, outdoing them all, Graham Robb's 'Sea-Green, Mad as a Fish'.[45] And, so that no one misses the point,

Antonia Fraser, in her review, draws 'a chilling lesson for us today': Robespierre was personally honest and sincere, but '[t]he bloodlettings brought about by this "sincere" man surely warn us that belief in your own righteousness to the exclusion of all else can be as dangerous as the more cynical motivation of a deliberate tyrant.'[46] Happy we who live under cynical public-opinion manipulators, not under the sincere Muslim fundamentalists ready to fully commit themselves to their projects . . . what better proof of the ethico-political misery of our epoch whose ultimate mobilizing motif is the mistrust of virtue! Should we not affirm against such opportunist realism the simple faith in the eternal Idea of freedom which persists through all defeats, without which, as was clear to Robespierre, a revolution 'is just a noisy crime that destroys another crime', the faith most poignantly expressed in Robespierre's very last speech on the 8 Thermidor 1794, the day before his arrest and execution:

> But there do exist, I can assure you, souls that are feeling and pure; it exists, that tender, imperious and irresistible passion, the torment and delight of magnanimous hearts; that deep horror of tyranny, that compassionate zeal for the oppressed, that sacred love for the homeland, that even more sublime and holy love for humanity, without which a great revolution is just a noisy crime that destroys another crime; it does exist, that generous ambition to establish here on earth the world's first Republic.[47]

SUGGESTED FURTHER READING

ROBESPIERRE TEXTS:

In English:
ROBESPIERRE Maximilien, *Speeches* (with a biographical sketch), New York, International Publishers, 1927.

In French:
ROBESPIERRE Maximilien, *Oeuvres*, edited by A. Soboul and M. Bouloiseau, Paris, 10 vols, 1958–67, (reprinted 2000 by Société d'Etudes Robespierristes (Paris); an eleventh volume of unpublished texts is in preparation).

Old but useful selections:
ROBESPIERRE Maximilien, *Textes choisis*, notes and introduction by Jean Poperen, Paris, Editions sociales, 3 vols, 1956-58 (reprinted 1974).
ROBESPIERRE Maximilien, *Discours et rapports à la Convention,* Paris, UGE 10/18, 1965.

A selection based on that by Jean Poperen, which is the most convenient to use:
ROBESPIERRE Maximilien, *Ecrits*, notes and introduction by Claude Mazauric, Paris, Editions sociales, 1989.

Two recent selections:
ROBESPIERRE Maximilien, *Pour le bonheur et pour la liberté. Discours*, selected and edited by Y. Bosc, F. Gauthier, S. Wahnich, Paris, La Fabrique, 2000.
ROBESPIERRE Maximilien, *Discours sur la religion, la République, l'esclavage*, Paris, Editions de l'Aube, 2006.

BIOGRAPHIES:

BOULOISEAU Marc, *Robespierre*, Paris, PUF, Que sais-je?, 1987.
JORDAN David P., *The Revolutionary Career of Maximilien Robespierre*, New York, Free Press, 1985.
MASSIN Jean, *Robespierre*, Aix-en-Provence, Alinéa, 1988.
SCURR Ruth, *Fatal Purity: Robespierre and the French Revolution,* London, Chatto and Windus, 2006.

STUDIES ON ROBESPIERRE AND THE TERROR:

ANDRESS David, *The Terror: The Merciless War for Freedom in Revolutionary France*, New York, Strauss and Giroux, 2006.
BRUNEL Françoise, *Thermidor, la chute de Robespierre*, Brussels, Editions Complexe, 1989.
GUENIFFEY Patrice, « Robespierre » in FURET F., OZOUF M., *Dictionnaire critique de la Révolution française*, Paris, Flammarion, 1988.
HAYDON Colin and DOYLE William (eds.), *Robespierre*, Cambridge, Cambridge University Press, 1999.
LABICA Georges, *Robespierre. Une politique de la philosophie*, Paris, PUF, 1990.
MATHIEZ Albert, *Etudes sur Robespierre*, Paris, Messidor, 1988.
MAYER, Arno, *The Furies: Violence and Terror in the French and Russian Revolutions*, Princeton, PUP 2002.
MAZAURIC Claude, « Robespierre », in SOBOUL A., *Dictionnaire historique de la Révolution française*, Paris, PUF, 1989.
SOBOUL Albert (ed.), *Actes du colloque Robespierre*, Paris, Société des études robespierristes, 1967.
WAHNICH Sophie, *La liberté ou la mort: essai sur la Terreur et le terrorisme*, Paris, La Fabrique, 2003.

GLOSSARY

Accapareurs: term used to refer to figures hated by the populace who could either be the administrators responsible for food supplies, or those who supported free trade in grain, and especially those who preferred to hoard their produce rather than to bring it to market (the latter could be sentenced to the death penalty from July 1793 onwards).

Committee of General Security: created under the Convention on 2 October 1792. Responsible for general and interior police matters, it entered into conflict with the Committee of Public Safety dominated by Robespierre.

Committee of Public Safety: created under the Convention on 6 April 1793, it was charged with taking measures of general internal and external defence. Robespierre began to sit on it from 27 July 1793 and continued to do so until his arrest. The powers of the Committee became more and more extensive, a process which created conflict with the Committee of General Security.

Constituent Assembly: founded at the Estates-General on 9 July 1789 and lasted until 30 September 1791. Robespierre was a member of this Assembly.

Convention: assembly elected by quasi-universal male suffrage, it succeeded the Legislative officially on 21 September 1792 with the beginning of the First Republic; first influenced by the Girondins (until 2 June 1793), then by the Montagnards with Robespierre playing a preponderant role (until 9 Thermidor Year II–27 July 1794), and finally by the Thermidorians (until 26 October 1795).

East India Company Affair: the decree of 24 August 1793 dissolved all joint stock companies. The liquidation of the East India Company was supposed to have been carried out by the state; when the decree was announced it emerged that the minutes had been been falsified with the complicity of Fabre d'Eglantine, who was then accused of corruption.

Federalism: designation for the delegates from the Girondin *départements* who were hostile to the authority of the Convention at the end of 1792–beginning of 1793.

Fédérés: the armies of the Revolution included battalions of *fédérés* who comprised a volunteer revolutionary force often mobilized to intervene against internal subversion. They played a decisive role in the fall of the monarchy on 10 August 1792.

Feuillants – Feuillantisme: the Feuillants Club was a split from the Jacobins at the time of the Champ-de-Mars affair (17 July 1791); it grouped together supporters of the constitutional monarchy, including La Fayette.

Girondins ('Brissotins'): 'Girondins' was the name given by the historiography of the nineteenth century to the supporters of Brissot and Vergniaud. During the Revolution they were known as 'Brissotins' or 'Rolandins' and they constituted the right wing of the Convention, favourable to economic liberalism and hostile to interventions by the popular movement.

Jacobin Club: first representing a moderate tendency, this society included a range of political figures in 1789: Mirabeau, La Fayette and Robespierre, among others. After a split away by the more moderate elements in 1791, the Club increasingly moved towards republican positions. The Girondins left it after the September Massacres of 1792 and thereafter it became a powerful centre for the Montagnards (see below). Closed after 9 Thermidor, it was reconstituted several times until its definitive dissolution in 1799.

Journées: The great *journées* of the Revolution were often synonymous with popular insurrections. The main ones were: 14 July 1789 (storming of the Bastille); 5–6 October 1789 (march of women on Versailles); 17 July 1791 (Champ-de-Mars Massacre); 10 August 1792 (fall of the monarchy); 31 May–2 June 1793 (fall of the Girondins), 9 Thermidor Year II (27 July 1794, fall of Robespierre).

Law of Suspects: the law of 17 September 1793 defined those suspected of being agents of the counter-revolution, principally priests, nobles and foreigners.

Maximum: the *sans-culottes* demanded a maximum price limit (to fight against speculators).

Montagnards: name given to the deputies sitting on the higher benches (the 'Mountain') of the Legislative Assembly and then of the Convention. They differed from the Girondins in drawing their support from the popular movement, by showing their support for regulation of the economy and finally by an equalizing vision of social relations. Robespierre was one of their most eminent representatives.

Paris Commune (also known as the Insurrectionary Commune): on 10 August 1792 an insurrectionary commune composed of members of the far left (Chaumette, Hébert) was formed. It took part in the great *journées* of the revolution but at the end of 1793 its power was supplanted by that of the Committee of Public Safety under the influence of Robespierre. Purged by the elimination of the Hébertists, it tried unsuccessfully to mobilize Paris to save Robespierre on 9 Thermidor.

Représentants en mission: members of the Convention who, from spring 1793 onwards, were sent alongside the armies and to the *départements*; they often played an important role in the local application of the Terror, although in a manner that varied greatly from individual to individual.

Revolutionary Government: on 10 October 1793 a report by Billaud-Varenne proclaimed the government as 'revolutionary until peacetime' (a decree specified the modalities on 18 November), meaning that the 1793 Constitution should only be applied in times of peace. This latter constitution was not put into practice and another – less democratic – one, that of Year III, succeeded it fourteen months after the fall of Robespierre.

Revolutionary Tribunal: set up in Paris in March 1793 by the Convention to judge the enemies of the Revolution, its power was extended thereafter notably with the law of the 'great Terror' (22 Prairial Year II–10 June 1794). It was suppressed several months after the fall of Robespierre on 31 May 1795.

Sans-culottes: originally a pejorative term, replacing that of *canaille*, for the lower classes. Literally the term refers to the absence of (aristocratic) knee breeches, thus indicating poverty and ignorance. With time, the term increasingly came to identify the 'people' as against the 'aristocrats'. For Robespierre, more than anything, it designated ardent patriots of modest origins.

Sections: originally, the sections in Paris simply had a role as electoral districts. As activists from the popular movement threw themselves increasingly into the sections, the latter tried to widen their scope of activity. With these organs thus gaining in autonomy, the Revolutionary Government progressively curtailed them.

Terror: term used to cover different measures taken by the state during the period from the summer 1792 to July 1794. Originally taken in a disordered manner, these measures became more systematic with the Convention's placing of the Terror on the 'order of the day' from 5 September 1793 onwards. The law of the 'Great Terror' of 22 Prairial Year II (10 June 1794) marked its climax. The repressive measures were indissociable from the context of internal and external warfare or from the economic measures aiming at greater equality.

Vendée: department in Western France which was the scene of an insurrection hostile to the Revolution – originally sparked off by the mobilization of 300,000 men for the armies – from March 1793 onwards. The insurrection was harshly repressed.

KEY FIGURES CITED IN THE TEXTS

Abbé Maury (Jean Siffrein) 1746–1817: elected to the Constituent Assembly, he was one of the principal defenders of the Ancien Régime against the Revolution. He emigrated to Rome in 1792.

Barère de Vieuzac (Bertrand) 1755–1841: deputy of the Constituent Assembly and then Montagnard deputy in the Convention. Member of the Committee of Public Safety, one of the organizers of the Terror; for a long time he was close to Robespierre but turned against him on 9 Thermidor.

Billaud-Varenne (Jean-Nicolas) 1756–1819: member of the Jacobin Club, he wrote texts in which he claimed to be a republican. Member of the Paris Commune after 10 August 1792, he then became a Montagnard deputy in the Convention and entered the Committee of Public Safety alongside Robespierre in September 1793, before becoming one of the instigators of 9 Thermidor.

Brissot (Jacques-Pierre) 1754–1793: member of the Jacobin Club, he contributed to the drafting of the petition calling for a republic which was carried to the Champ-de-Mars in July 1791. A deputy in the Legislative Assembly, he was one of the leaders of the Girondins and in favour of the war. Elected to the Convention, he opposed Robespierre and the Montagnards. He was tried and guillotined by the Revolutionary Tribunal.

Chaumette (Pierre Gaspard) 1763–1794: member of the Cordelier Club, he was the *procureur-syndic* of the Paris Commune in 1792. Robespierre opposed him on account of his de-Christianizing convictions. He was arrested and guillotined with the Hébertists.

Cloots (Anacharsis) 1755–1794: of Prussian origin, Cloots was in Paris and rallied to the Revolution in 1789. He named himself 'the orator of humanity' and he was a member of the Jacobins and a deputy in the Convention. A de-Christianizer, he was close to the Hébertists and was guillotined alongside them.

Danton (Georges Jacques) 1759–1794: a founder of the Cordelier Club in 1790, he became the Minister of Justice on 11 August 1792 after the fall of the monarchy. Elected to the Convention, he sat amongst the Montagnards. He was one of the instigators of the Terror but criticized virulently the Hébertist ultra-revolutionaries and, alongside other 'Indulgents', demanded an end to the Terror at the beginning of 1794. Implicated in a scandal, he was condemned to death and executed in April 1794 together with his supporters (including Camille Desmoulins).

Desmoulins (Camille) 1760–1794: member of the Cordelier Club and Montagnard deputy, he was close to Danton. At the end of 1793–beginning of 1794, he called for a softening of the Terror in his newspaper *Le Vieux Cordelier*. Condemned and executed in April 1794.

Dumouriez (Charles François du Périer) 1739–1823: member of the Jacobin Club, he became Minister for Foreign Affairs in March 1792 and then Commander in Chief of the armies of the North, winning the Battle of Valmy on 20 September 1792. During an offensive in March 1793, he was accused of treason and then handed over to the Austrians the agents sent by the Convention to keep an eye on him, before surrendering himself to the enemy.

Fouché (Joseph) 1759–1820: deputy in the Convention, he sat with the Montagnards. Charged alongside Collot d'Herbois with the repression of the federalists of Lyons, he distinguished himself by his ferocious application of the Terror. He was one of the instigators of the 9 Thermidor plot against Robespierre; thereafter, he became a loyal supporter of Bonaparte.

Hébert (Jacques René) 1757–1794: famous for his newspaper the *Père Duchesne*, he was Chaumette's substitute in the Paris Commune and a key figure in the Cordelier Club. He came into conflict with Robespierre, whom he accused of moderation on social questions, and was arrested and then condemned to death in March 1794.

La Fayette (Marquis de) 1757–1834: left for America in 1777 to help the insurgents and pushed the French government to support the anti-colonialists in the American War of Independence. Elected as a noble deputy in the Estates-General, he led the National Guard in July 1789. La Fayette wanted to reconcile the king and the Revolution, and was responsible for the shooting of demonstrators at the Champ-de-Mars. He then set up the Feuillants Club which supported a liberal monarchy and opposed the dethronement in 1792.

Marat (Jean-Paul) 1743–1793: member of the Cordelier Club, he became a deputy for Paris in the Convention and was famous for his newspaper *l'Ami du peuple* [*Friend of the People*] founded in September 1789. Sitting with the Montagnards, he became a hate figure for the Girondins who tried unsuccessfully to get him condemned by the Revolutionary Tribunal. He had a role in the sparking off of the September Massacres and especially in the overthrow of the Girondins. Assassinated on 13 July 1793 by Charlotte Corday, he became a cult figure amongst layers of the popular classes.

Priestley (Joseph) 1733–1804: important English chemist who supported the French Revolution; was accorded French citizenship and membership of the Convention.

Ronsin (Charles Philippe) 1752–1794: the author of a number of patriotic plays, he was a member of the Cordeliers and became General in Chief of the Parisian revolutionary army in September 1793. Fovourable to Hébert, he was executed alongside him and his supporters in March 1794.

Saint-Just (Louis Antoine) 1767–1794: deputy in the Convention, he sat alongside Robespierre and the Montagnards. Along with Couthon, Robespierre and Saint-Just formed a 'triumvirate' in the Committee of Public Safety. Very active in the factional struggle at the beginning of 1794, he tried to give the Terror a social edge with the 'Ventôse decrees'. Arrested and guillotined with Robespierre.

CHRONOLOGY

6 May 1758: Birth of Robespierre in Arras.

8 November 1781: Robespierre becomes a lawyer.

8 August 1788: Robespierre publishes his first political text: *A la nation artésienne* on the necessity of reform in the Estates of Artois.

1789

26 April: Robespierre elected as deputy of the Third Estate of Artois.

May – June: Robespierre joins the 'Breton Club', later known as the 'Jacobin Club'.

9 July: The Assembly proclaims itself the National Constituent Assembly.

14 July: Storming of the Bastille.

1790

31 March: Robespierre elected as President of the Jacobin Club for one month.

1791

17 July: Repression of the democratic movement on the Champ-de-Mars.

1 October: Opening of the Legislative Assembly.

1792

10 August: Overthrow of the monarchy and formation of the Insurrectionary Commune in Paris, of which Robespierre is a member.

2-6 September : Massacres in the prisons of Paris.

6 September: Robespierre elected deputy for Paris in the Convention.

20 September: Victory for the Republic at the Battle of Valmy.

21 September: Opening of the Convention. Beginning of the First Republic.

1793

21 January: Execution of Louis XVI.

10 March: Creation of the Revolutionary Tribunal.

31 May–2 June : Fall of the Girondins.

23–24 June: Passing of the Constitution.

27 July: Robespierre enters the Committee of Public Safety.

September: 'Terrorist' measures put on the agenda on 5 September 1793. Law of Suspects (17 September), the general maximum on prices and wages (29 September).

10 October: Government proclaimed 'revolutionary until peacetime'.

18 November (27 Brumaire Year II): Report presented by Billaud-Varenne on the functioning of the Revolutionary Government.

1794

4 February (16 Pluviôse Year II): Abolition of slavery in the French colonies.

26 February–3 March (8 and 13 Ventôse Year II): Saint-Just's Ventôse decrees.

14-24 March (24 Ventôse–4 Germinal): Trial and execution of the Cordeliers.

30 March–5 April (10–16 Germinal): Trial and execution of the 'Indulgents'.

8 June (20 Prairial): Festival of the Supreme Being.

10 June (22 Prairial): Law of the 'Great Terror'.

3 July (15 Messidor): Robespierre's last appearance at the Committee of Public Safety before Thermidor.

27 July 1794 (9 Thermidor Year II): Convention decrees the arrest of the Robespierrists after refusing Robespierre and Saint-Just the right to speak.

28 July 1794 (10 Thermidor Year II): Execution of the Robespierrists.

TRANSLATOR'S NOTE

It is not very surprising that the texts of most of Robespierre's speeches are available only from contemporary newspaper reports, or that they present variations and the occasional garbled passage. The men running revolutionary France, not just new to the job but trying to transform the way the job was done while learning how to do it, worked punishingly long hours. The situation, in the country and in the shifting new political institutions, changed by the day and often by the hour.

That sense of extreme urgency against a treacherously shifting background, of a man trying to do quite difficult things – for example, to define a working system of democracy that would not be a mere sham – at the same time as governing a country at odds with itself and its neighbours, does emerge from these texts. Their style is quite variable, some very clearly being more carefully worked than others.

The language itself gives some sense of the remoteness of 1790 France, post-Enlightenment but pre-modern. It is, though, the language of men who were helping to found modernity, to draw up a basic prototype of modern European – Western – humanity. Robespierre was a lawyer and often used legal expressions. It is not unusual in France to disparage him as an awkward and gauche orator, but when translating these texts I did not find them so. There was perhaps an effort on Robespierre's part to speak as a plain man, to avoid unnecessary flourishes and old-régime grandiloquence. Perhaps he chose to feature a provincial Artois twang, especially when uttering his considerable feats of sarcastic invective.

The new patriotism being promoted by the revolutionaries brought the word *la patrie*, whose nearest English equivalent is 'fatherland', into frequent use, and Robespierre uses it often. For people of my age, though, the word 'fatherland' has a tainted ring, and 'motherland' seems a gratuitous inversion. I have chosen to translate it as 'homeland'.

JH

NOTE ON TEXTS

In the selection and annotation of the following texts, full use has been made of the various French-language selections referred to in the Suggested Further Reading list, but in each case the full reference (volume and page numbers) to the version in Robespierre's *Oeuvres* is given.

All the notes were added by Jean Ducange.

Part One

ROBESPIERRE AT THE CONSTITUENT ASSEMBLY AND THE JACOBIN CLUB

Elected as a deputy to represent the Artois region at the Estates-General in April 1789, Robespierre spoke frequently in the Constituent Assembly. Alongside this, he was one of the first members of the Jacobin Club, where he made some of his most famous speeches.

The Legislative Assembly succeeded the Constituent Assembly in October 1791. The former deputies were excluded from the new assembly by a motion proposed by Robespierre himself.

Whilst many of these former deputies returned to the provinces and no longer played major political roles, Robespierre stayed in Paris at the tribune of the Jacobin Club.

I

ON VOTING RIGHTS FOR ACTORS AND JEWS

23 December 1789[1]

On 23 December, Robespierre intervened in the Constituent Assembly against Abbé Maury who had denounced the mores of actors. The latter were mostly excommunicated from the church under the Ancien Régime and deprived of any status defining their social position.

Two days earlier, Clermont-Tonnerre[2] had proposed that one's profession and faith should not render one ineligible for public office.

On 24 December, non-Catholics were conceded the right to hold public office, but Jews were not included. The latter gained the same rights as other citizens only on 27 September 1791.

Every citizen fulfilling the conditions of eligibility that you have prescribed has the right to public office. When you discussed those conditions, you were dealing with the great cause of humanity. The previous speaker tried to make three different causes out of a few specific circumstances. All three are contained in the principle, but for the sake of reason and truth, I am going to examine them briefly.

It will never be successfully claimed in this Assembly that a necessary function of the law can be stigmatized by the law. That law has to be changed, and the prejudice no longer having any basis will disappear.

I do not believe that you would need a law on the subject of actors. Those who are not excluded are eligible. It was good, however, that a member of this Assembly came to make a noise in favour of a class too long oppressed. Actors will merit public esteem more when an absurd prejudice no longer resists their obtaining it: then, the virtues of individuals will help to purify the shows, and theatres will become public schools of principles, good morals and patriotism.

Things have been said to you about the Jews that are infinitely exaggerated and often contrary to history. How can the persecutions they have suffered at the hands of different peoples be held against them? These on the contrary are national crimes that we ought to expiate, by granting them imprescriptible human rights of which no human power could despoil them. Faults are still imputed to them, prejudices, exaggerated by the sectarian spirit and by interests. But to what can we really impute them but our own injustices? After having excluded them from all honours, even the right to public esteem, we have left them with nothing but the objects of lucrative speculation. Let us deliver them to happiness, to the homeland, to virtue, by granting them the dignity of men and citizens; let us hope that it can never be policy, whatever people say, to condemn to degradation and oppression a multitude of men who live among us. How could the social interest be based on violation of the eternal principles of justice and reason that are the foundations of every human society?

2

ON THE SILVER MARK

April 1791[1]

The following speech was never delivered but was printed and discussed in the popular societies.

Robespierre is here opposing the distinction between 'passive' and 'active' citizens whereby only those able to pay a contribution equivalent to three days' work were eligible to vote. Moreover, only those able to pay a high tax – that is, a silver mark – were eligible to run for election.

Out of seven million (male) citizens, three million were thus excluded and considered as 'passive'. The Constitution of 1791 recognized this distinction, thus installing a qualified or restricted form of suffrage.

Quasi-universal male suffrage was only achieved with the fall of the monarchy and the election of the Convention.

Gentlemen,

I was in doubt, for a time, as to whether I should offer you my thoughts on some measures you appeared to have adopted. But I saw that it was a question of either defending the cause of the nation and of liberty, or betraying it by remaining silent; and I hesitated no longer. I even undertook this task with a confidence rendered all the more firm, in that the imperious passion for justice and the public good that imposed it on me was held in common with yourselves, and that it is your own principles and your own authority that I invoke in their favour.

Why are we gathered here in this temple of law? Doubtless, to enable the French nation to exercise the imprescriptible rights that belong to all men. Such is the object of every political constitution. It is just, it is free, if it fulfils that object; it is only an attack on humanity if it counters it.

You yourselves acknowledged this truth in a striking manner when, before starting your great work, you decided that these sacred rights, which are, as it were, the eternal foundations on which it should be based, ought to be solemnly stated.

'All men are born and remain free, and equal before the law.'

'Sovereignty resides essentially in the nation.'

'The law is the expression of the general will. All citizens have the right to contribute to its formation, either in person or through their freely elected representatives.'

'All citizens are eligible for all public offices, without any distinction other than their virtues and talents.'[2]

Those are the principles you established: it will be easy now to assess the provisions I mean to oppose; all that is needed is to compare them with those invariable rules of human society.

Now, firstly: is the law the expression of the general will, when the greater number of those for whom it is made cannot contribute to its formation in any way? No. But to deny to all those who do not pay a contribution equal to three working days the right to choose the electors intended to name the members of the Legislative Assembly, what else is that but ensuring that the majority of the French are absolutely excluded from the formation of the law? That provision is thus essentially anti-constitutional and antisocial.

Secondly: are men equal in their rights, when some enjoy exclusively the right to stand for election as members of the legislative body or other public institutions, others simply the right to appoint them, and the rest are deprived of all these rights? No. Such, however, are the monstrous differences established between them by decrees that render a citizen active or passive; or half active or half passive, depending on the various degrees of fortune enabling an individual to pay three working days, or ten days of direct taxation, or a silver mark. All these provisions are therefore essentially anticonstitutional and antisocial.

Thirdly: are men eligible for all public posts without distinction other than their virtues and talents, when the inability to discharge the required contribution disqualifies them from all public posts, whatever their virtues and talents may be? No; all these provisions are therefore essentially anticonstitutional and antisocial.

Fourthly: lastly, is the nation sovereign, when the greater number of the individuals who compose it are robbed of the political rights that constitute sovereignty? No; nevertheless you have just seen that these same decrees strip them away from the greater part of the French. What then would your Declaration of Rights be, if these decrees could survive?

An empty formula. What would the nation be? Enslaved; for liberty consists in obeying laws voluntarily adopted, and servitude in being forced to submit to an outside will. What would your constitution be? A veritable aristocracy. For aristocracy is the state in which one portion of the citizens is sovereign and the rest subjects. And what an aristocracy! The most unbearable of all, that of the rich.

All men born and domiciled in France are members of the political society called the French nation, in other words French citizens. That is what they are by the nature of things and by the main principles of the law of nations. The rights attached to this title depend neither on the fortune each individual possesses, nor on the amount of taxation to which he is subject, because it is not tax that makes us citizens; the quality of citizen only obliges him to contribute to the common expenditure of the state, according to his abilities. Now you can give laws to the citizens, but you cannot annihilate them.

The supporters of the system I am attacking have noticed this truth themselves since, not daring to contest the quality of citizen in the case of those they were disinheriting politically, they limited themselves to evading the principle of equality which it necessarily presupposes, by making a distinction between active citizens and passive citizens. Counting on the ease with which men are governed by words, they tried to put us off the scent by proclaiming, in this new expression, the most manifest violation of the rights of man.

But who could be so stupid as not to see that these words can neither change the principles, nor resolve the difficulty; since declaring that such citizens will not be active, and saying that they will no longer exercise the rights attached to the title of citizen, amount to exactly the same thing in the idiom of these subtle politicians. Now I will always ask them by what right they can thus strike their fellow-citizens and constituents with inactivity and paralysis: I will not stop clamouring against this insidious and barbaric locution, which will defile both our code and our language unless we hasten to erase it from both of them, in order that the word liberty does not itself become meaningless and derisory.

What shall I add to such obvious truths? Nothing for the benefit of the nation's representatives, whose opinions and wishes have already anticipated my demand: it just remains for me to answer the deplorable sophistries with which the prejudices and ambitions of a certain class of men strive to shore up the disastrous doctrine I am fighting; it is those men alone that I am now going to address.

The people! folk who have nothing! The dangers of corruption! The example of England, of peoples supposed to be free; these are the arguments deployed against justice and reason.

I ought only to answer with a word or two: the people, that multitude of men whose cause I am defending, have rights that come from the same origin as your own. Who gave you the power to take them away?

General practicality, you say! But is there nothing practical in what is just and honest? And does not that eternal maxim apply above all to social organization? And if the purpose of society is the happiness of all, the conservation of the rights of man, what should we think of those who want to base it on the power of a few individuals and the degradation and hopelessness of the rest of the human race! What then are these sublime politicians, who applaud themselves for their own genius, when by means of laborious subtleties they have at last managed to substitute their vain fantasies for the immutable principles graven in the hearts of all men by the eternal legislator!

England! ha! What good are they to you, England and its depraved constitution, which may have looked free to you when you had sunk to the lowest degree of servitude, but which it is high time to stop praising out of ignorance or habit! Free peoples! Where are they? What does the history of those you honour with this name show you? Other than aggregations of men more or less remote from the paths of reason and nature, more or less enslaved, under governments established by chance, ambition or force? So was it to copy slavishly the errors or injustices that have long degraded the human species that eternal providence called on you, on you alone since the world began, to re-establish on earth the empire of justice and liberty, in the heart of the brightest enlightenment ever to have illuminated public reason, amid the almost miraculous circumstances providence has been pleased to assemble, to supply you with the power to restore to mankind its original happiness, virtue and dignity?

Do they really feel the full weight of that sacred mission, those who, in answer to our justified complaints, are content merely to say coolly: 'With all its faults, our constitution is still the best that has ever existed.' Was it then so that you might nonchalantly leave in that constitution essential faults, destructive of the basic foundations of the social order, that twenty-six millions of men put the formidable weight of their destinies in your hands? Would it not be said that the reform of a great number of abuses and several useful laws would be so many favours granted to the people, enough to make it unnecessary to do any more in its interests? No, all the good you have done was a rigorous duty. The omission of good which you can do would be a breach of trust, the harm you would be doing a crime of *lèse-nation* and *lèse*-humanity. There is more: unless you do everything for liberty, you have done nothing. There are no two ways of being free: one must be entirely free, or become a slave once more. The least resource left to despotism will soon restore its power. What am I saying! it surrounds you already with its blandishments and its influence; soon it could overwhelm you with its force. You are pleased to have attached your names to a great change, but are not much concerned as to whether it is great enough to ensure human happiness. Make no mistake: the sound of the eulogies that astonishment and frivolity are causing to clamour about you will soon die down; posterity, comparing the greatness of your duties and the immensity of your resources with the fundamental flaws in your work, will say of you, with indignation: 'They could have made men happy and free; but they did not want to; they were unworthy of it.'

But, say you, the people! People who have nothing to lose! Will then be able, like us, to exercise the rights of citizens.

People who have nothing to lose! how unjust and false it is in the eyes of truth, that language of delirious arrogance!

The people of whom you speak are apparently men who live, who subsist, in society, without the means to live and subsist. For if they are provided with those means they have, it seems to me, something to lose or to preserve. Yes, the rough garments that clothe me, the humble garret to which I purchase the right to withdraw and live in peace; the modest wage with which I feed my wife, my children; these things, I admit, are not lands, carriages, great houses; all of them amount to nothing perhaps, to those accustomed to luxury and opulence, but they are something to ordinary humanity: they are sacred property, beyond doubt as sacred as the glittering domains of wealth.

What am I saying! My liberty, my life, the right to obtain safety or vengeance for myself and my loved ones, the right to repel oppression, to exercise freely all the faculties of my mind and heart, all these good things, so sweet, the first of those that nature has allotted to mankind, are they not entrusted, like yours, to the guardianship of the law? And you say I have no interest in this law; and you want to strip me of the share I should have, like you, in the administration of the state, for the sole reason that you are richer than I am! Ah! if the balance stopped being equal, should it not tend to favour the less prosperous citizens? The law, the public authority: is it not established to protect weakness against injustice and oppression? It is thus an offence to all social principles to place it entirely in the hands of the rich.

But the rich, the powerful, have reasoned differently. Through a strange abuse of words, they have restricted the general idea of property to certain objects only; they have called only themselves property owners; they have claimed that only property owners were worthy of the name of citizen; they have named their own particular interest the general interest, and to ensure the success of that claim, they have seized all social power. And we! oh human weakness! we who aspire to bring them back to the principles of equality and justice, it is still on the basis of these absurd and cruel prejudices that we are seeking, without being aware of it, to raise our constitution!

But what after all is this rare merit of paying a silver mark or some other tax to which you attach such high prerogatives? If you give the public Treasury a contribution more considerable than mine, is it not for the reason that society has given you greater pecuniary advantages? And, if we want to pursue this idea, what is the source of that extreme inequality of fortunes that concentrates all the wealth in a small number of hands? Does it not lie in bad laws, bad governments, and finally all the faults of corrupt societies? Now, why should those who are the victims of these abuses be punished again for their misfortune, by losing the dignity of being citizens? I envy not at all the advantageous share you have received, since this inequality is a necessary or incurable evil: but at least, do not take from me the imprescriptible property of which no human law can strip me. Indeed, allow me to be proud sometimes of an honourable poverty, and do not seek to humiliate me with the vainglorious pretension that the quality of sovereign is reserved for you, while I am left only with that of subject.

But the people! . . . the corruption!

Ah! stop, I say stop profaning the touching and sacred name of the people, by linking it with the idea of corruption. What is a person who, among men equal in rights, dares to declare his fellows unworthy of exercising theirs, and to take them away for his own advantage! And surely, if you allow yourselves to base such a conviction on assumptions of corruptibility, what a terrible power you are assuming over humanity! Where will your proscriptions end?

But is it really on those who do not pay the silver mark that they should fall, or on those who pay much more? Yes, in spite of all your bias in favour of the virtues that wealth brings, I dare say that you would find them as much in the class of the least-monied citizens as in that of the most opulent! Do you really believe in all honesty that a hard and laborious life produces more faults than softness, luxury and ambition? And have you less faith in the probity of our artisans and ploughmen, who under your tariff will almost never be active citizens, than tax-farmers, courtiers, those you used to call great lords, who under the same tariff would be active six hundred times over? I want one day to avenge those you call the people for these sacrilegious calumnies.

So are you fit to appreciate the people, and to know men, you who since reaching the age of reason have judged them only by the absurd ideas of despotism and feudal arrogance; you who, accustomed to the bizarre jargon invented by them, found it easy to denigrate the greater part of the human race with the words rabble and populace; you who have revealed to the world that there were people of no birth, as if all the men alive had not been born; as if there were not people risen from nothing who were men of merit, and gentlemen, respectable people who were the vilest and most corrupt of men. Oh, doubtless you can be permitted not to render the people all the justice that is due to it. For myself, I call on all those whom the instinct of a noble and sensitive soul has brought close to the people and made worthy to know and love equality, to witness that in general there is nothing so just or so good as the people, at all times when it is not irritated by excessive oppression; that it is grateful for the most trivial considerations shown to it, the slightest good done to it, and even for harm that is not done to it; that it is among the people that we find, beneath exteriors that we call rough, candid and upright souls, and a good sense and energy that one would seek long and in vain in the class that disdains it. The people asks only for what is necessary, it only wants justice and tranquillity, the rich aspire to everything, they want to invade and dominate everything. Abuses are the work and the domain of the rich, they are the scourges of the people: the interest of the people is the general interest, that of the rich is a particular interest; and you want to nullify the people and render the rich all-powerful!

Am I to hear again those eternal accusations that have been heaped continuously on it from the time when it was loosening the despots' yoke to the present, as if the entire people could be accused of a few specific and local acts of vengeance committed at the beginning of an unhoped-for revolution when, at last breathing freely after such long oppression, it was in a state of war with all its tyrants? What am I saying? What time has ever given such dazzling proof of its natural goodness as the moment when, armed with irresistible force, it suddenly held back of its own will and calmed down, at the request of its representatives? Oh you who show yourselves so inexorable towards suffering humanity, and so indulgent towards its oppressors, look at the history, glance around you, count the crimes of the tyrants, and judge between them and the people.

What am I saying? From the very efforts the enemies of the revolution made to slander it to its representatives, to slander you to it, to suggest to you measures designed to stifle its voice, or drain its energy, or mislead its patriotism, to prolong the neglect of its rights, by hiding your decrees from it, from the unfailing patience with which it has borne all its ills while awaiting a happier order of things, we should understand that the people is the sole support of liberty. Ah! who then could bear the idea of seeing it stripped of its rights, by the very revolution which is due to its courage, to the tender and generous affection with which it defended its representatives! Is it to the rich, is it to the great that you owe the glorious insurrection that saved France and saved you? Those soldiers who laid down their arms at the feet of the alarmed homeland, were they not of the people? And those who led them against you, to what classes did they belong? So, was it to help you defend its rights and its dignity that the people was then fighting, or was it to give you the power to annihilate them? Was it only to fall under the yoke of the aristocracy of wealth, that it joined you in breaking the yoke of the feudal aristocracy?

So far, I have accommodated myself to the language of those who seem to want to designate by the word people a separate class of men, to which they attach a certain idea of inferiority and contempt. It is time to speak with greater precision, by recalling that the system we are opposing proscribes nine-tenths of the nation, that it even removes from the list of those it calls active citizens a countless multitude of men whom even the prejudices of arrogance had respected, men distinguished by their education, their industry and even by their wealth.

Such in effect is the nature of that institution, that it leads people into the most absurd contradictions and that, taking wealth as the measure of citizens' rights, it departs from this very rule by linking them with what are called direct taxes, although it is obvious that a man who pays considerable indirect taxes may enjoy a bigger fortune than another who is only subject to a moderate direct tax. But how can anyone have thought of making the sacred rights of man depend on the mobility of financial systems, the variations, the motley forms that ours displays in different parts of the same state? What sort of system is it in which a man who is a citizen at one point on French territory, ceases to be one, either in whole or in part, when he moves to some other point; or one who is a citizen today ceases to be one tomorrow, if his fortune suffers a reverse!

What sort of system is it in which a decent man, robbed by an unjust oppressor, falls back into the class of helots,[3] while another is raising himself by crime to the rank of citizen! Or a father watches the certainty grow, along with the number of his children, that he will not be able to leave them this title with the small portion of their divided patrimony; or all the family sons, in half the empire, can only find a homeland when they no longer have a father! What use, finally, is this superb prerogative of membership of the sovereign, if the assessor of public contributions is in a position to take it from me, by reducing my contribution by one *sou*; if it is subject both to the caprices of men and the inconstancy of fortune?

And fix your attention especially on the disastrous problems it must inevitably cause. What powerful weapons will it not make available to intrigue!

How many pretexts given to despotism and aristocracy, for the removal from public assemblies of those men most needed for the defence of liberty, leaving the destiny of the state at the mercy of a certain number of rich and ambitious men! An early experience has already revealed to us all the dangers of this abuse. What friend of liberty and humanity did not groan on seeing, in the first elected assemblies formed under the auspices of the new constitution, the national representation reduced, so to speak, to a handful of individuals? What a deplorable spectacle we have been shown by those towns, those districts in which citizens disputed with citizens over the power to exercise rights common to all; where municipal officers, or people's representatives, by means of arbitrary and exaggerated assessments of the value of working days, appeared to be putting the highest possible price on the quality of active citizen! Let us not soon feel the baleful effects of these attacks on the people's rights! But it falls to you alone to prevent them. Even the precautions you have tried to take to soften the rigour of the decrees of which I speak, either by reducing the highest price of a day's work to twenty *sols*, or by admitting a number of exceptions; all these useless palliatives prove at least that you have felt for yourselves the full scale of the evil that your wisdom is destined to extirpate entirely. Well, what does it matter in effect whether twenty *sols* or thirty be the main element in the calculation that decides my political existence? Do not those who can only manage nineteen have the same rights? And the eternal principles of justice and reason on which those rights are based, can they be bent to the rules of a variable and arbitrary tariff?

Only look, I beg you, at the bizarre consequences that follow a great error of this sort. Forced by basic notions of equity to seek the means to palliate it, you have granted soldiers, after a certain length of service, the rights of active citizen as a reward. You have granted them as an honour to ministers of religion when they cannot fulfil the pecuniary conditions specified by your decrees; you will grant them again in analogous cases, from similar motives. Now, all these measures, so equitable in intent, are so many thoughtless acts and infractions of primary constitutional principle. How in fact, you who have abolished all privileges, how did you manage to establish the exercise of citizen's rights as a privilege for certain individuals and certain professions? How did you manage to change a benefit that belongs essentially to all, into a reward? And incidentally, if ecclesiastics and soldiers are not alone in deserving well of the homeland, should not the same reasoning force you to extend the same favour to the other professions? And if you reserve it for merit, how have you managed to make it a prerogative of wealth?

That is not all. You have made loss of the rights of an active citizen the penalty for a crime, and the greatest of all crimes, that of *lèse-nation*. This penalty seemed so great to you that you limited its duration, you left the culprits in a position to end it themselves, with the first public-spirited act it might please them to perform. And that same deprivation, you have inflicted on every citizen who is not rich enough to meet some specific size or nature of contribution; so that through the combination of these decrees, those who conspired against the salvation and liberty of the nation and the best citizens, defenders of liberty whom fortune has not favoured, or who may have neglected fortune to serve the homeland, are confounded in the same class. No, I am mistaken; your predilection is very plainly in favour of the first-mentioned; for from the moment they are really willing to make peace with the nation, and accept the benefit of liberty, they can return to the full enjoyment of citizen's rights; the others are deprived of them indefinitely, and can only recover them by fulfilling a condition which is not in their power. God in heaven! Genius and virtue placed lower than opulence and crime by the legislator!

If only he were still alive, we have sometimes said, when comparing the idea of this great revolution to that of a great man who contributed to its preparation! If only he were still alive, that sensitive and eloquent philosopher, whose writings developed among us the principles of public morality that made us capable of conceiving the plan to regenerate our homeland! Well, if he were still alive, what would he see? The sacred rights of man which he defended, violated by the new-born constitution; and his name erased from the list of citizens. And what would all those great men say, who once governed the most free and virtuous peoples on earth, but who did not leave enough to cover their funeral costs, and whose families were fed at the expense of the state? What would they say if, alive again among us, they could watch this much-vaunted constitution taking shape? O Aristides![4] Greece named you the Just and made you the arbiter of its destiny: regenerated France would see in you only an insignificant man who cannot pay a silver mark. In vain, the trust of the people would call on you to defend its rights; there is not a municipality that would not reject you. You might save the homeland twenty times over, and still not be an active citizen, or eligible . . . unless your great soul agreed to vanquish the rigours of fortune at the cost of your liberty, or of one of your virtues.

Those heroes were not unaware, and we repeat it ourselves sometimes, that the only solid foundation for liberty is morality. Now, what morals can a people have when its laws seem designed to encourage furious activity in the thirst for riches? And what more certain means of exacerbating that passion can the laws take, than to stigmatize honourable poverty, and reserve all the honours and all the power for wealth? Would the adoption of such an institution achieve anything but to force even the most noble ambition, the quest for glory through service to the homeland, to take refuge in cupidity and intrigue, and make the constitution itself the corrupter of virtue? So what does it signify, this civic list that you are putting up with such care? As I see it, it displays, with exactitude, all the names of the vile specimens that despotism fattened on the people's substance; but I search in vain for that of an indigent decent man. It gives the citizens this astonishing lesson: 'Be rich, whatever the cost, or you will be nothing.'

How, after that, could you flatter yourselves that you had revived among us the public spirit on which the regeneration of France depends, when by separating the greater part of the citizens from the cares of the state, you are condemning it to concentrate all its thoughts and all its affections on the objects of its personal interest and its pleasures; when, in other words, you are raising egoism and frivolity on the ruins of the useful talents and generous virtues that are the only guardians of liberty. There will never be a lasting constitution in any country where it is, in some sense, the domain of one class of men; and to the others only an uninteresting object, or a subject of jealousy and humiliation. If it be attacked by adroit and powerful enemies, it must succumb sooner or later. Already, gentlemen, it is easy to foresee all the deadly consequences that would follow the arrangements of which I speak, if they were allowed to subsist. Soon you will see your primary and elective assemblies deserted, not only because these same decrees forbid access to them by the greater number of the citizens, but also because most of those who are called, such as the three working days people, reduced to the condition of electors without themselves being able to be appointed to the jobs the citizens' confidence would give them, will be in no hurry to abandon their business and families to frequent assemblies in which they can have neither the same hopes nor the same rights as more comfortably off citizens; unless some of them go there to sell their votes. They will be abandoned to a small number of plotters who will share all the magistratures between themselves, and give judges, administrators, legislators to France. Legislators reduced to seven hundred and fifty for such a vast empire! who will deliberate, surrounded by the influence of a court armed with public powers, able to distribute a multitude of favours and jobs, and with a civil list that can be estimated as at least thirty-five millions. Look at it, that court, deploying its immense resources in every assembly, seconded by all those disguised aristocrats who, under the mask of public-spiritedness, seek to gather the votes of a nation still too idolatrous, too frivolous, too uninformed of its rights, to know its enemies, its interests and its dignity; watch it then trying to establish its deadly ascendancy over those members of the legislative body who have not arrived corrupted in advance and given over to its interests; watch it trifling with the destinies of France, with an ease that will not surprise those who for some time have followed the progress of its dangerous spirit and sinister intrigues, and be ready to watch despotism gradually degrade everything, deprave everything, absorb everything; or else hasten to give the people all its rights, and the public mind all the liberty it needs to expand and grow strong.

I end this argument here, perhaps I might even have managed to spare myself the trouble; perhaps I should have investigated, first of all, whether these measures I was attacking actually exist; whether they are real laws. Why should I fear telling the truth to the representatives of the people, why should I forget that defending before them the sacred cause of humanity, and the inviolable sovereignty of nations, with all the openness that requires, is both to flatter the sweetest of their feelings and to pay the most noble homage to their virtues? Besides, does not the universe know that your true wish, your true decree even, is the prompt revocation of the arrangements of which I speak; and that it is the opinion of the majority of the National Assembly that I am defending by fighting against them? So I declare it, decrees like that do not even need to be expressly revoked; they are essentially null and void, because no human power, not even yours, was competent to carry them through. The power of the representatives, the mandatories of a people, is necessarily determined by the nature and object of their mandate. Now, what is the object of your mandate? To make laws to restore and establish the rights of your constituents. It is thus not possible for you to strip them of those same rights. Give this your full attention: those who have chosen you, those through whom you exist, were not taxpayers of a silver mark, of three or ten days' work as direct taxes; they were all the French, that is all men born and domiciled in France, or naturalized, paying any tax at all.

Despotism itself had not dared to impose other conditions on the citizens it convened. How then could you despoil some part of these men, or rather the greater part of them, of those same political rights that they exercised by sending you to this Assembly, and with whose guardianship they entrusted you? You cannot do it without destroying your own power, since your power is only that of your constituents. In carrying through such decrees, you would not be acting as representatives of the nation: you would be acting directly against that title; you would not be making laws at all, you would be striking against the principle of legislative authority. Even peoples can never either authorize or adopt them, because they can never renounce equality, or liberty, or their existence as peoples, or the inalienable rights of man. So, gentlemen, when you have formed the already well-known resolution to revoke them, it will be less because you have recognized the need for it, than to set all legislators and all holders of public authority a great example of the respect they owe peoples; to crown so many salutary laws, so many generous sacrifices, with the magnanimous disavowal of a momentary aberration, which never made any difference either to your principles or to your steadfast and courageous devotion to human happiness.

So what is the meaning of the eternal objection that you are not permitted to change your own decrees under any circumstances? How did it happen that the inviolable rule that the salvation of the people and human happiness is always the supreme law was made to yield to that so-called maxim; and another imposed on the founders of the French constitution, one that would destroy their own work, and halt the glorious destinies of the nation and the whole of humanity, instead of repairing an error all of whose dangers they knew? It falls only to the essentially infallible Being to be immutable; to change is not just a right but a duty for any human will that has faltered. Men who decide the fate of other men are less exempt than anyone from this common obligation. But it is the misfortune of a people that moves rapidly from servitude to liberty to carry over to the new order of things, without being aware of it, the prejudices of the old order, which it has not yet had time to get rid of; and it is certain that this system of absolute irrevocability of decisions by the legislative body is just an idea borrowed from despotism. Authority cannot retreat without being compromised, it said, although in fact it has sometimes been forced to retreat. The maxim was good in effect for despotism, whose oppressive power could only shore itself up with illusion and terror; but the tutelary authority of the nation's representatives, based on both the general interest and the nation's strength, can repair a fatal error without risking any more than strengthening the feelings of confidence and admiration that surround it; it can only compromise itself by showing invincible perseverance in measures damaging to liberty and condemned by public opinion. There are, however, some decrees that you cannot abrogate, those that enshrine the Declaration of the Rights of Man; because it is not you who made those laws; you promulgated them. It is those immutable decrees of the eternal legislator, lodged in the minds and hearts of all men long before they were written into your code, that I call upon against measures that offend them, and that ought to disappear before them. You have here to choose between one and the other: and your choice cannot be uncertain, according to your own principles. I therefore propose to the National Assembly the following draft decree:

'The National Assembly, imbued with a religious respect for the rights of men, whose maintenance should be the object of all political institutions;

Convinced that a constitution designed to ensure the liberty of the French people, and to influence that of the world, ought to be established on that principle above all;

Declares that all Frenchmen, meaning all men born and domiciled in France, or naturalized, should enjoy fully and equally the rights of the citizen; and are eligible for all public office, without distinction other than that of their virtues and talents.'

3

ON THE CONDITION OF
FREE MEN OF COLOUR

13 May 1791 [1]

*On 13 May 1791, Moreau de Saint-Méry, a deputy from the French colony
of Martinique, proposed an amendment constitutionalizing slavery in the
overseas territories. Robespierre protested against this move. A few weeks later,
in August 1791, the slave rebellions began, sparking off a process that would
culminate in the abolition of slavery by the Convention on 4 February 1794.*

I have a very brief explanation of the amendment: gentlemen, the
greatest interest in this discussion is to produce a decree that does not
attack the principles and honour of the Assembly in too revolting a
manner.

The moment you pronounce, in one of your decrees, the word *slave*,
you will be pronouncing your own dishonour and the overthrow of
your constitution. I am complaining, in the name of the Assembly itself,
that not content with obtaining from it what they desire, they want to
force it to grant it in a way that would dishonour the Assembly, and that
contradicts your principles. When they tried to force you to lift,
yourselves, the sacred and terrible veil that the legislator's very modesty
had forced you to assume, I believe they may have wanted to give
themselves a means of always attacking your decrees with success, to
weaken your principles, so that they could always tell you: you are
endlessly citing the rights of man, the principles of liberty; but you
believed in them so little yourselves that you decreed slavery constitu-
tionally.

It is indeed a great interest, the conservation of your colonies, but even
that interest is connected with your constitution; and the supreme

interest of the nation and of the colonies themselves is that you conserve your liberty and do not overturn the foundations of that liberty with your own hands. Faugh! Perish your colonies, if you are keeping them at that price. Yes, if you had either to lose your colonies, or to lose your happiness, your glory, your liberty, I would repeat: perish your colonies.

I conclude from all this that the greatest misfortune that the Assembly could bring down, not on citizens of colour, not on the colonies, but on the entire French empire, would be to adopt the deadly amendment proposed by M. Moreau de St-Méry. I conclude that absolutely any other proposal, whatever it might be, would be worth more than that one.

4

ON THE RIGHTS OF SOCIETIES AND CLUBS

29 September 1791 [1]

Le Chapelier[2] presented a report to the Assembly which aimed at limiting the political activity of the clubs, which were considered a competing force. Robespierre opposed this orientation and defended the clubs' rights. Despite his intervention, the Assembly adopted the first articles of the report.

[. . .]

The revolution is over: I do want to suppose so with you, even if I do not fully understand the meaning you attach to that statement, which I have heard repeated with great affectation; but if the hypothesis is correct, is it then less necessary to propagate the knowledge, the principles of the constitution and of public-spiritedness, without which the constitution cannot subsist? Is it less useful to form assemblies in which the citizens can consider, in common, the most effective way of approaching such objectives and the most precious interests of their homeland? Is there any concern more legitimate and more worthy of a free people? For it to be true to say that the revolution is over, the constitution would need to have been consolidated, since the collapse and weakening of the constitution must necessarily prolong the revolution, which is nothing other than the nation's efforts to retain or acquire liberty. Now, how can anyone propose to nullify and render ineffectual the most powerful means of strengthening it, one that the rapporteur himself admits to have been generally recognized as necessary?

And where does it come from, this strange haste to remove all the props supporting an edifice that is still poorly buttressed? What is this scheme to try and plunge the nation into deep inertia concerning the most sacred of its interests, to forbid the citizens to have any sort of anxieties, when everything suggests that it is still not demented to have some; to treat as criminal the watchfulness that reason imposes even on peoples that have enjoyed liberty for centuries past?

To me, when I see on one hand that the nascent constitution still has internal and external enemies, when I see that the talk and the external signs have changed but the actions are still the same, and hearts can only have changed through a miracle; when I see intrigue, duplicity sounding the alarm and at the same time sowing trouble and discord, when I see the heads of opposing factions fighting less for the revolutionary cause than to encroach on the power to rule under the name of monarch; when on the other hand I see the exaggerated zeal with which they prescribe blind obedience, at the same time as proscribing even the word liberty; and see the extraordinary means they use to kill public-spiritedness by reviving prejudice, frivolity, idolatry, far from condemning those around me for the drunken spirit that animates them, I see it only as a spirit of vertigo propagated by the slavery of nations and the despotism of tyrants. [*Applause*] If those who share the cares of legislators are regarded as dangerous men; if I am not convinced that people who think like that are senseless, imbecilic, I am forced to see them as traitors. If I must stop speaking out against the plans of enemies of the homeland, if I must applaud the ruin of my country, give me any orders you want, and let me perish before the loss of liberty: [*Applause, murmurs*] as well there will still be men in France who are sincere enough friends of liberty, perceptive enough to detect all the traps set for us on all sides, to prevent traitors from ever enjoying the fruit of their efforts.

I know that to ensure the success of the projects today being offered for your deliberation, care was taken to lavish criticisms, sophistries, calumnies and all the small means employed by the small men who are both the shame and the curse of revolutions. [*Applause, laughter in the centre*] I know they have converted to their opinions everything France has that is nasty and foolish. [*Laughter*] I know that projects of this sort are very pleasing to all men interested in prevaricating with impunity; for any man who can be corrupted fears the scrutiny of informed citizens, as brigands fear the light that exposes their crimes. Nothing but virtue can foil this sort of conspiracy against the patriotic societies. Destroy them, and you will have removed the most powerful brake on corruption, you will have overturned the last obstacle standing in the way of these sinister plans;

for the conspirators, the plotters, the ambitious, will be perfectly capable of assembling, will be well able to elude the law they have had pronounced; they will know how to rally under the auspices of despotism to reign in its name, and they will be rid of the societies of free men who assemble peaceably and publicly under common rights, because it is necessary for surveillance by honest people to stand against the forces of ambitious and corrupt intriguers. Then they will be able to tear the country apart with impunity and cultivate their personal ambition on the ruins of the nation. Gentlemen, if circumstances from the past could now be recalled to your minds in a clear manner, you will remember that these societies were composed of men who were most commendable for their talents, their zeal for the liberty they have conquered; that they met in them to prepare in advance to fight in this very Assembly against the league of enemies of the revolution, to learn how to foil the traps that plotters have been setting for us until this very moment. If you remember all the circumstances, you will see with as much surprise as pain that this decree is perhaps instigated by the personal insult that was offered to certain individuals who had acquired too much influence over the public opinion that now rejects them.

Is it then such a great misfortune if, in our present circumstances, public opinion and public spirit are developing at the expense of a few men who served the cause of the homeland in appearance, only to betray it with greater boldness? [*Applause, murmurs*]

I know just how harsh my frankness is; but the only consolation left to good citizens for the danger in which these men have put the state is to judge them in a severe manner.

The patriotic societies have been represented to you as having usurped public power, when really they have never had the ridiculous aspiration to interfere with the constituted authorities, when really they have never had any goal but to inform, to enlighten their fellow-citizens on the true principles of the constitution, and to spread the enlightenment without which it cannot survive. If some societies have strayed from the rules prescribed by the law, well! The law is there to repress those particular departures; but do we wish to infer from a few isolated acts, for which no proof has been given, the conclusion that it is necessary to destroy, paralyse, annihilate entirely an institution useful in itself, needed for the maintenance of the constitution, and which, as even its enemies admit, has rendered essential services to liberty? If there is a hideous spectacle, it is that of a representative assembly willing to sacrifice the security of the constitution to the interests of a few individuals devoured by passions and ambition.

I limit myself to asking the preliminary question about the Committee's proposal, and I leave to those who wish to oppose my opinion the task of refuting me with wonderfully ingenious jokes and Machiavellian artistry . . . [*Applause from the left and the public galleries*].

5

EXTRACTS FROM 'ON THE WAR'

2 January 1792[1]

Whilst the probability of conflict with other nations seemed to be receding, Brissot, the leader of the 'Brissotins' (Girondins), intervened in the Legislative Assembly in favour of war. On 29 December, he maintained that 'the war is necessary to France for her honour [. . .] The war is a national benefit'. On 30 December, he spoke of a 'crusade of universal liberty'. Here, Robespierre replies to Brissot in a speech to the Jacobin Club which began on 2 January 1792 and was concluded at a session on 11 January.

[. . .] Shall we make war or shall we make peace? Shall we attack our enemies, or shall we wait for them at home? I believe that this wording does not express the question in all respects or to its full extent. What position should the nation and its representatives adopt in the circumstances we are in now, towards our internal and external enemies? That is the real point of view from which it should be seen, if we want to assimilate it in its entirety and discuss it with all the exactitude it deserves. What matters, above all else, and whatever the fruit of our efforts may be, is to enlighten the nation on its true interests and those of its enemies; not to deprive liberty of its last resource, by misleading the public mind in the present critical circumstances. I will attempt to meet this objective by responding mainly to the opinion of M. Brissot.

If a few broad strokes, if the brilliant and prophetic painting of a war ending in fraternal embraces from all the peoples of Europe are sufficient arguments to decide such a serious question, I will concur that M. Brissot has resolved it perfectly; but his speech seemed to me to display a vice that is negligible in an academic discourse, but that is of some importance in the greatest of all political discussions; this is that he has ceaselessly avoided the fundamental point of the question, to erect his entire system off to the side on an absolutely ruinous foundation.

Of course I like the idea of a war undertaken to extend the reign of liberty just as much as M. Brissot, and I too could surrender to the pleasure of recounting all its marvels in advance. Were I the master of France's destinies, could I but direct its forces and its resources at will, I would long ago have sent an army to Brabant, I would have helped the Liégeois and smashed the fetters of the Batavians;[2] these expeditions are much to my taste. But I would absolutely not, to tell the truth, have declared war on rebellious subjects. I would even have deprived them of the will to assemble;[3] I would not have allowed enemies who are more formidable and closer to us to protect them and give rise to more serious dangers within.

But given the circumstances in which I find my country, I cast an anxious glance about me, and I wonder whether the war to be waged will be the one that enthusiasm promises us; I ask myself who is proposing it, how, in what circumstances, and why?

That – our wholly extraordinary situation – is where the whole question resides. You have unceasingly looked away from it; but I have proved what was clear to everyone, that the proposal for the present war was the outcome of a plan formed long ago by internal enemies of our liberty; I have shown you its aim; I have pointed out its means of execution; others have proved to you that it was just an obvious trap: one orator, a member of the Constituent Assembly, has spoken truths on this matter that are in fact very important;[4] there is no one who would not have spotted this trap, considering that it was after constantly protecting the rebel emigrations and emigrants that people were proposing to declare war on their protectors, at the same time as continuing to defend the internal enemies confederated with them. You have yourselves acknowledged that the war was pleasing to the émigrés, that it pleased the ministry, the Court intriguers, that numerous faction whose leaders, only too well known, have directed every step taken by the executive power; all the trumpets of the aristocracy and the government are sounding the signal for it in unison; finally, anyone who could believe that the conduct of the Court, since the beginning of this revolution, has not been steadfastly opposed to the principles of equality and respect for the people's rights, would be regarded as a madman, if he meant it in good faith; anyone who could say that the Court would suggest a measure as decisive as war, without relating it to its own plans, would not be giving a much better impression of his judgement. Now, can you say it makes no difference to the good of the state whether the enterprise of war is led by the love of liberty or the spirit of despotism, by loyalty or perfidy? Yet what did you reply to all these decisive facts? What did you say to dissipate such well-founded suspicions? Your response to the fundamental principle of this whole discussion calls your entire system in question.

'Distrust,' you said in your first speech, 'distrust is a frightful state: it prevents the two powers from acting in concert; it prevents the people from believing in demonstrations by the executive power, cools its attachment, reduces its submissiveness.'[5]

Distrust is a frightful state! Is that the language of a free man who believes that no price is too high for liberty? It prevents the two powers from working in concert! Is it still you who are speaking here? What! It is the people's distrust that prevents the executive power from functioning; and it is not its own will? What! It is the people who ought to believe blindly in the *demonstrations* of the executive power; and it is not the executive power that ought to merit the people's trust, not through *demonstrations*, but through deeds? *Distrust cools its attachment*! So to whom does the people owe attachment? To a man? To the work of its hands, or to the homeland, to liberty? *It reduces its submissiveness*! To the law, no doubt. Has that been lacking until now? Who has the more reasons for self-reproach in this respect, the people or its oppressors? That text caused me some surprise, and I confess that it did not diminish when I heard the commentary with which you developed it in your last speech.

You informed us that distrust needed to be banned because there had been a change in the ministry.[6] What! You, who possess philosophy and experience, you, whom I have heard twenty times saying, on the politics and the immortal spirit of courts, all that any man having the faculty of thought thinks on the subject; it is you who claim that the ministry ought to change with a minister! I am in a position to explain myself freely on the subject of ministers: firstly because I do not fear being suspected of speculating on their succession, either for myself or for my friends; secondly because I have no desire to see them replaced by others, being convinced that those who aspire to their jobs would be worth no more than they are. It is not ministers that I am attacking; it is their principles and their actions. Let them change, if they can, and I will fight their detractors. I have the right, therefore, to examine the foundations of the endorsement you are giving them. You blame Minister Montmorin who ceded his place, to transfer public confidence to Minister Lessart who has taken over his role! God forbid that I should waste precious moments in drawing a parallel between those two illustrious defenders of the people's rights! You dispatched two certificates of patriotism to two other ministers, for the reason that they had been drawn from the the the class of plebeians,[7] but I say quite frankly that the most reasonable assumption, in my opinion, is that in our present circumstances *plebeians* would never have been called to the ministry if they had not been thought worthy of being nobles. I am astonished that a representative of the people should place confidence in a minister whom the people of the capital feared to see given a municipal post; I am astonished to see you recommending to the public goodwill the Minister of Justice,[8] who paralyzed the provisional court of Orleans,[9] by refraining from sending it the important cases; the minister who grossly slandered the country's patriotic societies in front of the National Assembly, to bring about their destruction; the minister who, more recently, asked the present Assembly to suspend the establishment of the new criminal courts, on the pretext that the nation was not yet ripe for juries, on the pretext (who would believe it!) that winter is too rough a season to establish this institution, declared an essential part of our constitution by the constitutional act, demanded by the eternal principles of justice, and by the unbearable tyranny of the barbaric system that still weighs down on patriotism and on humanity; that minister, the oppressor of the Avignonnais people, surrounded by all the intriguers you yourself have denounced in your writings, and the declared enemy of all patriots steadfastly attached to the public cause. You have also taken under your protection the present Minister of War. Ah! For pity's sake, spare us the effort of discussing the conduct, the connections and the staff of so many individuals, when the only questions should concern principles and the homeland. Not content with eulogizing these ministers, you then want to isolate them from the views and society of men who are notorious for being their advisers and collaborators.

No one doubts today that there is a powerful and dangerous alliance against equality and against the principles of our liberty; it is known that the coalition which laid sacrilegious hands on the foundations of the constitution is actively pursuing the means to complete its work; that it is dominant at court, that it controls ministers; you have admitted that it had a plan to extend ministerial power still further, and to aristocratize national representation; you have begged us to believe that the ministers and the court had nothing in common with it; you have contradicted, in this connection, the vigorous assertions of several speakers and general opinion; you thought it enough to allege that a few plotters could not harm liberty in the slightest. Are you unaware that it is plotters who do real harm to peoples? Are you unaware that a few plotters, backed by the force and treasure of the government, are not to be ignored? That you yourself once made a law to prosecute with energy some of those we are talking about here? Are you unaware that since the king's departure, whose mystery is starting to become clearer, they have had the power to make the revolution retreat, and to commit with impunity the most reprehensible attacks on liberty? Where has it come from all of a sudden, all this indulgence, or this feeling of security?

Do not be alarmed, the same speaker has told us, if this faction wants war; do not be alarmed if the court and the ministers want war too; or if the papers, *bribed by the ministry*, are preaching war: ministers, to tell the truth, will always side with moderates against patriots; but they will side with moderates and patriots against the émigrés. What a reassuring, what a luminous theory! Ministers, you admit, are the enemies of patriots; the moderates, for whom they have declared themselves, want to make our constitution aristocratic; and you want us to adopt their plans? Ministers, as you yourself say, are bribing some newspapers whose job is to extinguish the public mind, to efface the principles of liberty, to sing the praises of its most dangerous enemies, to slander all good citizens; and you want me to trust the views and principles of these ministers?

You believe that agents of the executive power are more disposed to adopt the maxims of equality, and defend the people's rights in all their purity, than to compromise with members of the dynasty, with friends of the Court, at the expense of the people and the patriots whom they openly call agitators? But aristocrats of every stripe are demanding war; all the aristocracy's toadies are repeating the war cry: so probably, no one should doubt their intentions. For myself, I admire your good luck and do not envy it. Your destiny was to defend liberty without distrust, without displeasing its enemies, without finding yourself in opposition to the court, or the ministers, or the moderates. How easy and smiling the paths of patriotism have become for you!

Speaking for myself, I have found that the further one advanced in this career, the more obstacles and enemies one encountered, the more often one was deserted by people with whom one had started out; and I must confess that if I saw myself like that, surrounded by courtiers, by aristocrats, by moderates, then I should be tempted at the very least to think I was in fairly bad company.

If I am not mistaken, the weakness of the reasons with which you have tried to reassure us on the intentions of those who are pressing for war, is very striking evidence that can prove them conclusively. Far from approaching the real state of the question, you have always avoided it. Everything that you have said is therefore beside the point. Your opinion is based on nothing but vague and foreign hypotheses.

[. . .] It is in the nature of things that the march of reason should be slow and gradual. The most depraved government finds powerful support in the prejudices, the habits, the education of peoples. Despotism even corrupts men's minds to the point of making them adore it, to the point of making liberty appear suspect and frightening at first sight. The most extravagant idea that can arise in the mind of a politician is the belief that a people need only make an armed incursion into the territory of a foreign people, to make it adopt its laws and its constitution. No one likes armed missionaries; and the first counsel given by nature and prudence is to repel them as enemies. [. . .]

Before losing yourselves in the politics and the states of the princes of Europe, start by turning your gaze to your internal position; restore order at home before carrying liberty abroad. But you claim that this task should not even concern you, as if the ordinary rules of common sense did not apply to great politicians. Restoring order in our finances, halting the depredations that afflict them, arming the people and the national guards, doing all the things this government has tried to prevent so far, so that we may fear neither the attacks of our enemies, nor ministerial intrigues; reviving through beneficent laws, through a character sustained by energy, dignity and wisdom, the public mind and the horror of tyranny, the only things that can make us invincible against all our enemies: all of those are just ridiculous ideas; war, war, as soon as the court asks for it; that tendency dispenses with all other concerns, you are even with the people the moment you give it war; war on fugitives from the national court, or on German princes; trust, idolatry, for the enemies within. But what am I saying? Do we have them, any enemies within? No, you don't know of any, you only know about Koblenz.[10] Did you not tell us that the seat of evil is in Koblenz? So it is not in Paris? So there is no connection between Koblenz and another place that is not far from here? What! You dare to say that what has set the revolution back is the fear inspired across the nation by fugitive aristocrats it has always despised;

and yet you expect of this nation prodigies of every kind! Learn then that in the judgement of all enlightened Frenchmen, the real Koblenz is in France; that the one in the bishopric of Trier is but one of the supports of a widespread conspiracy being hatched against liberty, and whose home, whose centre, whose leaders are among us. If you do not know that, you are a stranger to all that is happening in this country. And if you do know it, why do you deny it? Why distract public attention from our most formidable enemies, to fix it on other objects, to lead us into the trap where they are waiting for us?

Some others, who are vividly aware of the depth of our ills, and know their true cause, are evidently mistaken on the remedy. In a sort of despair, they want to hurl themselves into a foreign war, as if they hoped that the mere change brought about by war would bring us to life, or that order and liberty would eventually emerge from the general confusion. They are committing the most disastrous of errors, for they do not discern the circumstances, and confuse ideas that are absolutely distinct. There are in revolutions movements contrary to liberty and movements that favour it, as in illnesses there are salutary crises and mortal ones.

The favourable movements are those aimed directly against tyrants, like the Americans' insurrection, or that of 14 July. But war on the outside, provoked, directed by the government in the circumstances we are in now, is a movement in the wrong direction, a crisis that could lead to the death of the body politic. Such a war can only send public opinion off on a false scent, divert the nation's well-founded anxieties, and forestall the favourable crisis that attacks by enemies of liberty might have brought on. It was from that angle that I first argued against the drawbacks of this war. During a foreign war the people, as I said, distracted by military events from political deliberations affecting the essential foundations of its liberty, is less inclined to take seriously the underhand manoeuvres of plotters who are undermining it and the executive government which is knocking it about, and pay less attention to the weakness or corruption of representatives who are failing to defend it. This policy has been known since the beginning of time, and whatever M. Brissot may have said, the example I cited of the Roman aristocrats is strikingly relevant. When the people demanded its rights against the usurpations of the Senate and patricians, the Senate would declare war, and the people, forgetting its rights and resentments, would concentrate on nothing but the war, leaving the Senate its authority and preparing new triumphs for the patricians. War is good for military officers, for the ambitious, for the gamblers who speculate on these sorts of event; it is good for ministers, whose operations it covers in an impenetrable, almost sacrosanct veil; it is good for the court, it is good for the executive power whose authority, whose popularity and ascendancy it augments; it is good for the coalition of nobles, plotters, moderates who govern France. This faction can place its heroes and members at the head of the army; the court can entrust the forces of the state to men who, when the time comes, can serve its interests with greater success, because a sort of reputation for patriotism will have been worked up for them; they will win over the hearts and the trust of the soldiers only to attach them more strongly to the cause of royalism and moderation; that is the only seduction I fear where the soldiers are concerned, for I need no reassurance as to the likelihood of their deserting the public cause openly and voluntarily. The sort of man who would look with horror on the betrayal of the homeland can still be led by adroit officers to run its best citizens through with steel; the perfidious words republican and agitator, invented by the sect of hypocritical enemies of the constitution, can turn deceived ignorance against the people's cause. Now, the destruction of the patriotic party is the great objective of all their plots. It is not a counter-revolution that I fear, it is the advance of false principles, of idolatry, and the loss of public spirit. Now do you believe it would be a trivial advantage for the court and the party of which I speak to confine the soldiers, put them in camps, divide them into army corps, isolate them from the citizens, so as to substitute imperceptibly, under the imposing names of military discipline and honour, that spirit of blind and absolute obedience, the old military spirit, for the love of liberty, the popular sentiments that had been maintained by their communication with the people? Although the spirit in the army may still be good in general, should you really conceal from yourselves the fact that intrigue and suggestion have had some success in several corps, and that it is no longer entirely what it was in the first days of the revolution? Do you not fear the system steadily followed for so long, for bringing the army round to a pure love of kings, and for purging it of the patriotic spirit, which seems always to have been regarded as a plague that would ravage it? Can you behold without some small anxiety the minister's travels and the nomination of some general famous for disasters involving the more patriotic regiments?[11] Do you count for nothing the arbitrary power of life and death with which the law will invest our military patricians, from the moment the nation settles on war?

Do you count for nothing the police authority that will be given to the military chiefs of all our frontier towns? Have all these facts been answered with a dissertation on the Roman dictatorship, and the parallel between Caesar and our generals? It has been said that the war would intimidate the aristocrats within, and would cut off the source of their operations; not at all; they know the intentions of their secret friends too well to fear the outcome; they will be the more active in pursuing the veiled war that they can wage on us with impunity, by sowing division, fanaticism, and by corrupting opinion. It is then that the moderate party, clothed in the liveries of patriotism, whose leaders are the architects of this scheme, will deploy its sinister influence to the full; it is then that in the name of public security they will impose silence on anyone who might dare to voice some slight suspicions on the conduct or intentions of the agents of the executive power on which the moderate party is based, of the generals who will have become, like it, the hope and the idol of the nation. If one of these generals should happen to achieve some sort of apparent success, which will not, I believe, prove very damaging to the emigrants, or deadly to their protectors, what ascendancy will he not provide for his party? What services will he not be able to render to the court? It is then that a more serious war will be waged on the true friends of liberty, and that the perfidious system of egoism and intrigue will triumph. Once the public mind has been corrupted, then how far will the executive power and the factions serving it not be able to extend their usurpations? There will be no need to compromise the success of these plans with imprudent haste; perhaps there will be no hurry to propose the plan of action that has already been discussed: it could be that one or another could be adopted; what can (the party) not expect from time, from listlessness, ignorance, internal divisions, manoeuvres by the extensive cohort of its accomplices in the legislative body, in a word from all the components it has been preparing for so long?

Our generals, you say, will not betray us; and if we were betrayed, so much the better! I will not tell you that I find this taste for betrayal singular; for I am in perfect agreement with you on that. Yes, our enemies are too adept to betray us openly, as you expect; the kind of betrayal we have to fear, which I have just spelt out to you, that kind does nothing to alert public vigilance, it prolongs the slumber of the people until the moment the shackles go on; that kind leaves no expedient untried; all those who lull the people to sleep favour its success; and take good note that to achieve it, there will not even be any need to make war seriously; it is enough to put us on a war footing, it is enough to give us the idea of a foreign war; even if no other advantage was gained from it but the millions being counted in advance, it will not have been wholly wasted effort. Those twenty millions, especially at the present moment, have at least as much value as patriotic addresses in which confidence and war are preached to the people.

I am discouraging the nation, you say. No; I am enlightening it; to enlighten free men is to awaken their courage, to prevent that courage itself from becoming a stumbling-block to their liberty; and if I should turn out to have done nothing more than expose so many traps, than refute so many false ideas and defective principles, than stop outbursts of dangerous enthusiasm, then I will have advanced the public mind and served the homeland. [. . .]

Part Two

IN THE NATIONAL CONVENTION

On 6 September 1792, Robespierre was elected to the Convention by the electors of the capital.

From the end of 1792 to the first months of 1793, he concentrated his attacks against the 'Brissotins', who were expelled from the Convention following the 'journées' of 31 May and 2 June 1793.

On 27 July 1793, he entered the Committee of Public Safety, whose principal decisions he would not only often defend in public, but in which he was also the moving spirit until May 1794.

6

EXTRACTS FROM 'ANSWER TO LOUVET'S ACCUSATION'

5 November 1792[1]

During the autumn of 1792, Robespierre had to face the attacks of the Girondins at the Convention. One of them, Jean-Baptiste Louvet, a brilliant orator, claimed that Robespierre wanted to install a dictatorship. The latter responded in a speech that had a powerful impact inasmuch as it legitimated the popular initiatives from 10 August 1792 onwards, which marked the fall of the monarchy and the creation of an Insurrectionary Commune of which Robespierre was a member.

[. . .] But let us come to positive evidence. One of the most terrible reproaches made against me, I make no effort to hide it, is the name Marat.[2] I am going to start by telling you candidly what were my relations with him; I can even make a profession of faith on the subject, but without saying anything better or worse about him than I think, for I will not misrepresent my own thought to flatter general opinion. In January 1792, Marat came to see me. Before that time I had had no relations of any kind with him, direct or indirect. The conversation ran on public affairs, of which he spoke to me with despair. For my part I told him all that the patriots, even the most ardent, thought of him; to wit, that he had himself created an obstacle to the good that might come from the useful truths developed in his writings, by insisting on forever returning to extraordinary and violent propositions (for example the assertion that five or six hundred guilty heads should roll), which revolted the friends of liberty as much as they did the aristocracy. He defended his opinion; I persisted in mine; and I must confess that he found my political views so narrow that some time later, when he resumed publishing his journal[3] after abandoning it for a while, when giving an account of the conversation I have just described, he wrote baldly that on leaving me he had been perfectly convinced that I had *neither the views, nor the boldness of a statesman*; and if Marat's criticisms could be seen as favourable endorsements, I could still show you a couple of his sheets, published six weeks before the last revolution, in which he accused me of Feuillantism,[4] because, in a periodical publication, I was not saying openly that the constitution should be overturned.

Since that first and only visit from Marat, I have seen him in the electoral assembly. Here I rejoin M. Louvet, who accuses me of having designated Marat as a deputy; of having spoken ill of Priestley;[5] and finally, of having dominated the electoral assembly through intrigue and through fear [. . .]

Before ending this article, just tell us what you mean by those two portions of the people that you separate in your speeches and reports, one of which is fawned on, adulated and led astray by us, while the other is peaceable, but intimidated; one of which cherishes you, while the other seems to lean towards our principles. Would your intention here be to designate both those that La Fayette[6] called honest folk, and those he named *sans-culottes* and rabble?

There remains the most fertile and the most interesting of the three chapters of your defamatory address, the one that concerns my conduct on the General Council of the Commune.[7]

In the first place, I am asked why, after resigning from the post of public prosecutor, I accepted the title of municipal officer.

The answer is that I resigned the lucrative, and far from perilous whatever people may have said, post of public prosecutor in January 1792, and accepted the functions of a Commune council member on 10 August 1792. The very manner in which I entered the room where the new municipality was sitting is seen as criminal; and my accuser has reproached me very seriously for having walked towards the committee: in those conjunctures, when other concerns were pressing for our attention, I had no idea that I would one day be obliged to inform the National Convention that I had gone to the committee simply to verify my powers. From all these facts M. Louvet deduced no less than an assurance that the General Council, or several of its members at least, were reserved for high destinies. Could you doubt it? Was it not a fairly high destiny in itself, dedicating oneself to the homeland? Personally, I am proud of having to defend here both the Commune's cause and my own. But I can only rejoice in the fact that a large number of citizens have served the state better than I have. I have absolutely no wish to lay claim to a glory that is not mine. I had only just been named on the 10th; but those who, chosen sooner, were already assembled at the Commune building, on the fateful night, at the moment when the court conspiracy was ready to break out: those are really the heroes of liberty. It was they who served as rallying points for the patriots, armed the citizens, directed the movements of the tumultuous insurrection on which public salvation depended, and frustrated treason by arresting the commander of the National Guard, in the pay of the court, after convicting him, on written evidence in his own hand, of having ordered the commanders of security battalions to allow the insurgent people to pass, then to shoot them down from behind . . . Citizens, although most of you were unaware of these facts, which occurred well out of your sight, it is important for you to know them, if only so that you will not tarnish the representatives of the French people with an ingratitude fatal to the cause of liberty; you should hear them with interest at least, so that it may not be said that here only denunciations are welcomed as of right.

Is it so difficult then to understand that in such circumstances, this much-slandered municipality needed to include the most generous citizens? In it were those men disdained by monarchical baseness, because they only have strong and sublime souls; in it, as we saw, both in the citizens and in the new magistrates, were qualities of heroism that lies from those devoid of civic spirit will struggle in vain to erase from history.

Intrigues disappear along with the passions that gave birth to them; great deeds and great characters stand alone. We do not know the names of the vile agitators who assailed Cato[8] with stones in the Roman people's forum, and the gaze of posterity rests only on the sacred image of that great man.

Would you like to judge the revolutionary General Council of the Paris Commune? Then place yourselves at the heart of the immortal Revolution that created it, and of which you are yourselves the product.

You have been incessantly reminded, since you met, of the likelihood that plotters had introduced themselves into this body. I know that a few did exist in fact; and who has more right to complain about them than I have? They are among my enemies. And besides, what body was ever so pure and so few in number as to be absolutely exempt from that scourge?

A few reprehensible acts, imputed to some individuals, are being perpetually denounced to you. I know nothing of these deeds; I neither deny them nor believe them; for I have heard too many calumnies to believe denunciations that come from the same source and that all bear the imprint of bias or passion. I will not even tell you that the man on that General Council whom people are most keen to compromise is necessarily devoid of these characteristics; I will not stoop so low as to observe that I was never put in charge of any kind of commission, I was never involved, in any way, with any specific operation; that I never presided over the Commune for a single moment; that I never had the slightest relation with the surveillance committee, now so much slandered.[9] For on weighing it all up, I would consent willingly to be charged with all the good and all the bad attributed to that body, which has been so often attacked for the purpose of indicting me personally.

The new municipality is blamed for arrests that are called arbitrary, although none has been made without an interrogation. After the Roman consul stifled Catalina's conspiracy, Clodius accused him of violating the law.[10] When the consul gave an account of his administration to the people, he swore that he had saved the state, and the people applauded. I have seen citizens at this bar, who are not Clodiuses, but who had the prudence to take refuge in Rouen some time before the 10 August revolution, emphatically denouncing the conduct of the council of the Paris Commune. Illegal arrests! So is it with criminal code in hand that we must assess the salutary precautions needed for public safety in times of crisis, brought on by the very impotence of the law? Might you not also reproach us for having illegally smashed the mercenary scribblers, whose profession was to propagate fraud and blaspheme against liberty?[11] Might you not start a commission to list the grievances of aristocratic and royalist writers? Could you not reproach us for having put all the conspirators out through the gates of this city? Could you not reproach us for having disarmed suspect citizens, for having expelled known enemies of the revolution from our assemblies, where we were deliberating on public safety? Perhaps you could put on trial, all at once, the municipality and the electoral assembly and the Paris sections and the primary assemblies in the cantons, and all those who have imitated us? For all those things were illegal: as illegal as the Revolution, as the overthrow of the throne and the Bastille, as illegal as liberty itself.

But what am I saying? What I have just presented as an absurd hypothesis is actually a very certain reality. We have in effect been accused of all those things, and many others besides. Were we not accused of sending, in concert with the executive council, commissioners into several departments, to propagate our principles and persuade them to unite with the Parisians against the common enemy?

So what idea have people formed of the recent revolution? Did the overthrow of the throne appear so easy before the event? Was it just a matter of a surprise raid on the Tuileries? Was it not necessary to annihilate the tyrants' party throughout France and, to that end, communicate to all the departments the salutary commotion that had just electrified Paris? And how could that task not involve the magistrates who had called the people to insurrection? It was a matter of public safety, their heads were at stake! And they are called criminal for having sent commissioners to other communes, to persuade them to acknowledge, to consolidate their work! What am I saying! Calumny has pursued those same commissioners; some have been clapped in irons. Feuillantism and ignorance exaggerated the vigour of their approach, measured all their steps with constitutional compasses, to find a pretext to travesty the missionaries of the Revolution as incendiaries and enemies of public order. Hardly had the circumstances which had constrained the enemies of the people ceased when those same administrative bodies, all the men who were conspiring against the people, came forward to slander them to the National Convention itself.

Citizens, did you want a revolution without a revolution? What is this spirit of persecution that has come to revise, so to speak, the one that broke our chains? But what sure judgement can one make of the effects that can follow these great commotions? Who can mark, after the event, the exact point at which the waves of popular insurrection should break? At that price, what people could ever have shaken off the yoke of despotism? For while it is true that a great nation cannot rise in a simultaneous movement, and that tyranny can only be hit by the portion of citizens that is closest to it, how would these ever dare to attack it if, after the victory, delegates from remote parts could hold them responsible for the duration or violence of the political torment that had saved the homeland? They ought to be regarded as justified by tacit proxy for the whole of society. The French, friends of liberty, meeting in Paris last August, acted in that role, in the name of all the departments. They should either be approved or repudiated entirely. To make them criminally responsible for a few apparent or real disorders, inseparable from so great a shock, would be to punish them for their devotion. They would have a right to say to their judges: 'If you repudiate the means we have employed to prevail, leave us the fruits of victory. Take back your constitution and all your old laws; but restore to us the price of our sacrifices and our battles; give us back our fellow-citizens, our brothers, our children, who have died for the common cause.'

Citizens, the people whose envoys you are has ratified everything. Your presence here is the proof; it has charged you not with casting a severe inquisitorial eye on facts that touch on the insurrection, but with consolidating through just laws the liberty the insurrection gave it. The universe, posterity, will see in these events only their sacred cause and their sublime outcome; you should see them like that. You should judge them, not as justices of the peace, but as statesmen and legislators for the world. And do not think that I have invoked these eternal principles because we need to cover up or veil some few reprehensible acts. No, we had no need for that at all, I swear it by the overturned throne, and by the rising Republic.

You have heard a great deal of the events of 2 September.[12] That is the subject I was most impatient to arrive at, and I will deal with it in an absolutely disinterested manner. I observed that on reaching this part of his address, M. Louvet himself generalized, in a very vague way, the accusation directed earlier against me personally; from this it seems certain that calumny had been doing its work in the shadows. Those who have said that I had the smallest part in the events of which I speak, are either excessively credulous men, or excessively perverse ones: and as for the man who, anticipating the success of the defamation whose whole scheme he had planned in advance, thought he could then print with impunity that I had actually directed them, I would happily leave him to his remorse, if remorse did not presuppose the possession of a soul. I will say, for those who might have been misled by the fraud, that before the time when the events occurred, I had ceased to attend the General Council of the Commune; the electoral assembly, of which I was a member, had started its sittings; and I only learned of what was happening in the prisons by public rumour, and later no doubt than the greater part of the citizens; for I was either at home, or in the places to which I was summoned by my public functions. As for the General Council of the Commune, it is also certain, in the eyes of any impartial man, that far from provoking the events of 2 September, it did everything in its power to prevent them. If you are wondering why it did not prevent them, I am going to tell you. To form an accurate idea of these events, the truth should be sought, not in the writings or slanderous speeches that have misrepresented them, but in the history of the recent revolution.

If you thought that the change imprinted on people's minds by the August insurrection had wholly expired at the beginning of September, you were mistaken; those who have sought to persuade you that there was no analogy between one of these periods and the other, were feigning to know neither the facts nor the human heart [. . .]

However, a new and much more important cause brought the fermentation to its peak. A large number of citizens had thought that the 10 August revolution snapped the strings of the royal conspiracies, and regarded the war as over, when suddenly the news spread in Paris that Longwy had been surrendered; that Verdun had been surrendered; and that leading an army of a hundred thousand men, Brunswick was advancing on Paris.[13] No strong redoubt separated us from the enemy; our army divided, almost destroyed, by La Fayette's treachery, lacked everything; we had to think about finding weapons, camping equipment, food and men, all at the same time. The executive council did not hide either its fears or its difficulties. The danger was great; it appeared greater still.

Danton, speaking before the Legislative Assembly, gave an urgent account of the dangers and the resources available, persuaded it to take a few vigorous measures and gave a broad impetus to public opinion.[14] He visited the Commune, and invited the General Council to have the tocsin rung. The General Council of the Commune felt that the homeland could only be saved by the prodigies that enthusiasm for liberty alone can generate, and that the whole of Paris needed to set off and rush towards the Prussians. It had the tocsin rung to warn all the citizens to arm themselves; it procured weapons for them by every means in its power; the alarm cannon was discharged as well: in a moment, 40,000 men had been armed, equipped, assembled and marched towards Châlons . . . Amid this general movement, the approach of foreign enemies reawakened the feelings of indignation and vengeance that still smouldered in people's hearts, against the traitors who had called [the enemy] in. Before leaving their hearths, their wives and children, the citizens, the victors of the Tuileries, wanted to see the punishment of the conspirators that had so often been promised; people rushed to the prisons . . . Could the magistrates stop the people? For this was a popular movement, not the partial sedition of a few scoundrels paid to assassinate people of their own kind, as has been ridiculously supposed.

Well, if it had not been like that, how is it that the people did not stop it? How is it that the National Guard, how is it that the *fédérés*[15] did not make a single move to oppose it?[16] The *fédérés* themselves were present in large numbers.[17] We know that the commander of the National Guard made vain efforts to assert control; we know that commissioners from the national Legislative Assembly were sent to the prisons and that their efforts were in vain.

I have heard a number of people telling me coolly that the municipality should have proclaimed martial law.[18] Martial law, with the enemy approaching! Martial law, after 10 August! Martial law, against the people, to protect the accomplices of a dethroned tyrant! What could the magistrates do against the determined will of an indignant people, which countered their speeches with the memory of victory and its devoted readiness to hurl itself towards the Prussians, and which blamed the law itself for the prolonged impunity of traitors who were tearing at the flesh of their homeland. Unable to persuade the people to leave the task of punishing them to the courts, the municipal officers insisted that they follow prescribed forms whose aim was to avoid any confusion between those they wanted to punish, and citizens imprisoned for reasons unconnected with the 10 August conspiracy; and it is the very municipal officers who exercised this office – the only service that circumstances permitted them to render humanity – who have been described to you as bloodthirsty brigands!

Not even the most ardent zeal for the execution of the laws can justify exaggeration or calumny; I can quote here, against M. Louvet's declamations, testimony that is above suspicion, that of the Minister of the Interior who, while condemning popular executions in general, was not afraid to mention the spirit of prudence and justice which the people – that was his expression – showed on that occasion. What am I saying? I could quote, in favour of the General Council of the Commune, M. Louvet himself, who began one of his *Sentinelle* posters[19] with the words: 'Honour to the General Council of the Commune; it sounded the tocsin, and saved the homeland'. That was at the time of the elections.

We are assured that an innocent person perished; some have taken pleasure in exaggerating the number; but even one is too many, beyond doubt. Citizens, weep for that mistake. We have long wept for it: he was a good citizen, they say, so he was one of our friends. Weep even for the guilty victims, subject to the law's vengeance, who fell to the blade of popular justice; but let your grief come to an end, like all human things.

Let us keep back some tears for more touching calamities. Weep for a hundred thousand patriots immolated by tyranny; weep for our fellow-citizens expiring under their blazing roofs, and the sons of citizens massacred in the cradle, or in their mothers' arms. Have you not also brothers, children, wives of your own to avenge? The family of French legislators is the homeland; it is the human race as a whole, less the tyrants and their accomplices. Weep then, weep for humanity crushed under their odious yoke; but be consoled if, silencing all the base passions, you want to ensure the happiness of your country and of the world; be consoled, if you want to recall exiled equality and justice to earth, and make just laws to dry up the wellspring of the crimes and misfortunes of your fellows.

A sensibility that wails almost exclusively over the enemies of liberty seems suspect to me. Stop shaking the tyrant's bloody robe in my face, or I will believe that you wish to put Rome in chains. Looking at the touching paintings of calamities besetting the Lamballes[20] and Mon-tmorins,[21] of the consternation of the bad citizens, and those furious rantings against men widely regarded in a completely different way, did you not feel you were reading a manifesto from Brunswick or Condé?[22] Eternal slanderers, do you wish then to avenge despotism? Do you want to sully the cradle of the Republic? Do you want to dishonour the Revolution that gave it birth in the eyes of Europe, to give ammunition to all enemies of liberty? A truly admirable love of humanity, one that tends to consolidate the misery and servitude of peoples, and veils a barbaric desire to wallow in the blood of patriots! [. . .]

[. . .] But let us leave the circle of infamies through which you have led us, and arrive at the conclusion of your libel. Independently of that decree on armed force that you seek to extort by so many means; independently of that tyrannical law against individual liberty and freedom of the press that you disguise under the specious pretext of provocation to murder, you are demanding, for the minister, a sort of military dictatorship; you are demanding a law to proscribe citizens who displease you, under the name of ostracism. So you no longer blush at confessing openly the shameful reason for all these impostures and machinations. So you only talk about dictatorship in order to exercise it yourself without any restraint; you only talk about proscriptions and tyranny because you want to proscribe and tyrannize. So you thought that to make the National Convention the blind instrument of your culpable designs, you had only to recite a cunning romance to it, and then without stopping suggest that it decree the ruin of liberty and its own dishonour.

What remains to be said against accusers who accuse themselves? If possible, let us bury these despicable manoeuvres in eternal oblivion. If we could but hide from the gaze of posterity those inglorious days of our history when the people's representatives, duped by feeble intrigues, seemed to forget the great destiny to which they had been called! For myself, I draw no conclusion that might be personal to me. I have given up the facile advantage of answering the slanders of my adversaries with even more formidable denunciations. I have tried to suppress the offensive part of my justification. I renounce the just vengeance I would have a right to pursue against the slanderers; I ask that that vengeance be nothing more than the return of peace and the triumph of liberty. Citizens, resume, with a firm and rapid step, your superb career; and would that I may, at the cost of my life and very reputation, join with you in bringing glory and happiness to our common homeland!

7

EXTRACTS FROM 'ON SUBSISTENCE'

2 December 1792[1]

*In autumn 1792, a serious economic crisis led to a rise in the cost of living.
Unrest developed with demands for taxation measures. Robespierre intervenes
in this speech to promote the limitation of property rights,[2] or, more precisely,
their subordination to the right of existence.*

To address the people's representatives on ways of providing for its
subsistence is to address them not only on the most sacred of their duties
but also the most precious of their interests. For they surely identify
themselves with the people.

I do not mean to plead only the cause of indigent citizens, but that of
property-owners and tradespeople too.

I will limit myself to recalling a few obvious principles, but ones that
seem to have been forgotten. I will refer only to simple measures that
have already been proposed, for the task here is not so much to create
brilliant theories as to return to the primary notions suggested by
common sense.

In every country where nature provides for the needs of men with
prodigality, scarcity can only be imputed to defects of administration or
of the laws themselves; bad laws and bad administration have their origins
in false principles and bad morals.

It is a fact generally recognized that the soil of France produces a great
deal more than is needed to feed her inhabitants and that the present
scarcity is an artificial one. The conclusion to be drawn from this fact and
the principle I have stated may be awkward, but this is no time to flatter
ourselves. Citizens, it is you who will have the glory of making genuine

principles prevail, and giving the world just laws. You are certainly not here to plod servilely along the rut of tyrannical prejudices traced by your predecessors; rather you are starting a new career in which no one has preceded you. You need at least to subject to severe examination all the laws made under royal despotism and under the auspices of noble, ecclesiastical or bourgeois aristocracy; and so far you have no others at all. The most imposing authority being cited is that of a minister of Louis XVI, fought by another of the same tyrant's ministers.[3] I saw the birth of the Constituent Assembly's legislation on the grain trade; it was just the same as in the period that preceded it; and it has still not changed, because the interests and prejudices that were its foundations have not changed at all. I saw, during the time of that Assembly, the same events that are now occurring once again; I saw the aristocracy accuse the people; I saw hypocritical intriguers attributing their own crimes to defenders of liberty whom they called agitators and anarchists; I saw an impudent minister, whose virtue it was not permitted to question, demanding worship from France while ruining her, and from the centre of those criminal intrigues saw tyranny emerge, armed with martial law, to wallow legally in the blood of starving citizens. Millions to the minister from whom it was forbidden to ask for accounts, subsidies that went into the pockets of leeches on the people, unlimited freedom of trade, and bayonets to calm fears or appease hunger: such was the vaunted policy of our first legislators.

Subsidies can be discussed; freedom of trade is necessary up to the point where homicidal greed starts to abuse it; the use of bayonets is an atrocity; the system is essentially incomplete, because it fails to touch on the real principle.

The errors into which we have fallen on this matter seem to me to come from two main causes.

Firstly, the authors of the theory treated foodstuffs essential for life as ordinary merchandise, and made no distinction between the trade in wheat, for example, and the trade in indigo; they had far more to say about the grain trade than about the subsistence of the people; and having failed to bring that fundamental matter into their calculations, they made a faulty application of generally obvious principles; that mixture of true and false added something specious to an erroneous system.

Secondly, they did even less to adapt it to the stormy circumstances that revolutions bring; and their vague theory, even if it had been good for ordinary times, would have no application to the instantaneous measures that moments of crisis can require of us. They counted for much the profits of merchants or landowners, and the lives of men for almost nothing. And why? It was great men, ministers, the rich who were writing, who governed; had it been the people, it seems probable that this system would have been given a few modifications!

Common sense indicates, for example, the truth that foodstuffs that are in no way essential to life can be left to untrammelled speculation by the merchant; any momentary scarcity that might be felt is always a bearable inconvenience; and it is acceptable in general that the unlimited freedom of such a market should turn to the greater profit of the state and some individuals; but the lives of men cannot be subjected to the same uncertainty. It is not necessary that I be able to purchase brilliant fabrics; but I do need to be rich enough to buy bread, for myself and my children. The merchant is welcome to retain goods coveted by wealth and vanity in his shops, until he finds the moment to sell them at the highest possible price; but no man has the right to amass piles of wheat, when his neighbour is dying of hunger.

What is the first object of society? It is to maintain the imprescriptible rights of man. What is the first of those rights? The right to life.

The first social law is therefore the one that guarantees all members of society the means to live; all the others are subordinate to that one; property was only instituted and guaranteed to consolidate it; it is primarily to live that people have property. It is not true that property can ever be in opposition to human subsistence.

The foods necessary to man are as sacred as life itself. Everything essential to conserve life is property common to the whole of society. Only the surplus can be individual property and left subject to the enterprise of merchants. Any mercantile speculation I make at the expense of my fellow's life is not trade at all, it is brigandage and fratricide.

Under this principle, what is the problem that needs to be solved on this matter of legislation on subsistence? It is this: to guarantee to all members of society the enjoyment of that portion of the fruits of the earth which is necessary for their existence, and to landowners or cultivators the price of their industry, while yielding the surplus to freedom of trade.

I defy the most scrupulous defender of property to contest these principles, short of declaring openly that he understands this word as the right to despoil and assassinate his fellows. So how have people been able to claim that any sort of restriction, or rather any regulation of the trade in wheat, was an attack on property, and disguise that barbaric system under the specious name of freedom of trade? Do the authors of this system not perceive that they are inevitably in contradiction with themselves?

Why are you forced to approve the prohibition of grain exports whenever abundance is not assured in the interior? You yourselves fix the price of bread; do you fix that of spices, or of the brilliant products of India? What is the cause of all these exceptions, if it is not the very obviousness of the principles I have just developed? What am I saying? Sometimes the government even subjects the trade in luxury goods to modifications dictated by sound policy; why should the one affecting the people's subsistence be compulsorily exempt?

No doubt if all men were just and virtuous; if cupidity were never tempted to devour the people's substance; if the rich, receptive to the voices of reason and nature, regarded themselves as the bursars of society, or as brothers to the poor, it might be possible to recognize no law but the most unlimited freedom; but if it is true that avarice can speculate on the misery and tyranny itself on the despair of the people; if it is true that all the passions declare war on suffering humanity, then why should not the law repress these abuses? Why should it not stay the homicidal hand of the monopolist, as it does that of the common murderer? Why should it not concern itself with the subsistence of the people, after caring so long for the pleasures of the great, and the power of despots?

Now, what are the means of repressing these abuses? It is claimed that they are impracticable; I maintain that they are as simple as they are infallible; it is claimed they present an insoluble problem, even to genius; I maintain that at least they present no difficulty to common sense and good faith; I maintain that they injure neither the interests of commerce, nor the rights of property.

Let the circulation of goods be protected throughout the whole Republic; but let the necessary measures be taken to ensure that circulation takes place. It is precisely the lack of circulation that I am complaining about. For the scourge of the people, the source of scarcity, is the obstacles placed in the way of circulation, under the pretext of rendering it unlimited. Does public subsistence circulate when greedy speculators are keeping it piled in their granaries? Does it circulate, when it is accumulated in the hands of a small number of millionaires who withhold it from the market, to make it more valuable and rare; who coldly calculate how many families must perish before the commodity reaches the release date fixed by their atrocious avarice? Does it circulate, when it merely crosses the regions where it is produced, before the eyes of indigent citizens suffering the tortures of Tantalus,[4] to be swallowed up in the unknown pit of some public scarcity entrepreneur? Does it circulate when alongside the most abundant harvests the needy citizen languishes, unable to give a gold piece or a slip of paper valuable enough to obtain a bag of it?

Circulation is that which puts the essential foodstuff within reach of all men, and carries abundance and life into humble cottages. Does blood circulate when it is congested in the brain or in the chest? It circulates when it flows freely through the body; subsistence is the blood of the people, and its free circulation is no less necessary to the social body than that of the blood to the life of the human body. So support the free circulation of grain, by preventing all harmful congestions. By what means is this object to be achieved? By depriving cupidity of the motive and facility to bring them about. The three things that favour them are: secrecy, undefined freedom, and the certainty of impunity.

Secrecy, when anyone can hide a quantity of public subsistence of which he is depriving the whole of society; when he can fraudulently cause it to vanish and transport it either to foreign countries or to inland warehouses. Now, two simple measures are proposed: the first is to take the necessary steps to record the quantity of grain that each area has produced, and that each landowner or farmer has harvested. The second consists in forcing grain merchants to sell the grain on the market, and forbidding all transportation of purchases during the night. Neither the practicability nor the usefulness of these measures needs to be proved; for neither is contested. Is that legitimacy? But how in any case could general police regulations, made in the interests of society, be seen as an attack on property? Ha! what sort of good citizen can complain of being obliged to act with probity and in broad daylight? To whom are the shadows necessary, other than conspirators and knaves? Besides, have I not proved to you that society had the right to demand the portion that is necessary for the subsistence of the citizens? What am I saying? This is the most sacred of its duties. How then could the laws necessary to ensure its fulfilment be unjust?

I said that the other causes of the disastrous operations by the monopoly were undefined liberty and impunity. What surer way of encouraging greed and detaching it from any sort of brake, than to state as a principle that the law has not even the right to supervise it, to subject it to the lightest of curbs? That the only rule prescribed for it is the power to try anything, with impunity? What am I saying? Such is the degree of perfection to which this theory has been carried that it is all but established that hoarders are impeccable; that monopolists are benefactors of humanity; that in the quarrels that arise between them and the people it is the people who are always in the wrong. Either the crime of monopoly is not possible or it is real. If it is a chimera, how come that people have always believed in that chimera? Why have we been suffering its ravages since the first moment of our revolution? Why do believable reports and incontestable facts point to its culpable manoeuvres? And if it is real, through what strange privilege does it alone obtain the right to be protected? What limits would the pitiless vampires who speculate in human misery set to their attacks, if any kind of protest was invariably met with bayonets and the absolute command to believe in the purity and beneficence of all hoarders? Undefined liberty is none other than the excuse, the safeguard and the cause of this abuse. How then could it be its cure? What is being complained of? Precisely those evils that the present system has produced, or at least evils that it has not managed to prevent. And what remedy is proposed to us? The present system. I denounce the assassins of the people to you, and you reply: let them be. Under this system, everything is against society; everything favours the grain merchants.

Here, legislators, all your wisdom and all your circumspection are needed. Such a subject is always delicate to deal with; it is dangerous to add to the alarm of the people and to seem even to be authorizing its discontent. It is still more dangerous to silence the truth and to dissimulate principles. But if you are willing to observe them, all difficulties evaporate; only principles can stem the source of the evil.

I am well aware that when we examine the circumstances of some particular riot, aroused by the real or imagined scarcity of wheat, we sometimes recognize the influence of an outside cause. Ambition and intrigue need to start trouble: sometimes it is those same men who stir up the people, to find the pretext to slaughter it and to make liberty itself seem terrible in the eyes of weak and selfish individuals. But it is no less true that the people is naturally upright and peaceable; it is always guided by a pure intention; the malevolent can only stir it up by presenting a motive that is powerful and legitimate in its eyes. They make use of its discontent rather than whipping it up; and when they lead it into ill-considered acts, through the pretext of subsistence, they can do so only because it is receptive to such impressions, from oppression and misery. A contented people was never a turbulent people. Anyone who knows men, and especially anyone who knows the French people, also knows that it is not in the power of a madman or a bad citizen to make it rise for no reason against the laws that it loves, still less against its chosen representatives and against the liberty it has conquered. It is for those representatives to show the same confidence in it that it places in them, and to frustrate aristocratic malevolence, by satisfying its needs and calming its fears.

Even the fears of the citizens ought to be be respected. How can they be calmed, if you remain inactive? The very measures being proposed, even if they are less necessary than we think, the mere fact that the people desires them, that they prove your attachment to its interests, should be enough to persuade you to adopt them. I have already mentioned the nature and spirit of these laws, and will limit myself here to asking that any draft decrees that propose precautions against monopoly be given priority, while reserving the right to suggest modifications should they be adopted. I have already proved that these measures and the principles on which they are based were necessary to the people. I am now going to prove that they are useful to the rich and to all property owners.

I would take from them no honest profit, no legitimate property; I would take from them only the right to infringe on those of others; I would not destroy commerce at all, only the monopolist's brigandage; I would sentence them only to the punishment of allowing their fellows to live. Now nothing, really, could be more advantageous to them; the greatest service the legislator can perform for men is to force them to be honest folk. The greatest interest of man is not to accumulate treasure, and the sweetest property is certainly not to devour the subsistence of a hundred poor families. The pleasure of comforting his fellows, and the glory of serving his homeland, are worth at least as much as that deplorable advantage. What use to the greediest speculators is the undefined freedom of their odious trade? It makes them either oppressed or oppressors. The latter destiny is especially frightful. Rich egoists, learn to foresee and avert in good time the terrible results of the struggle of pride and limp passions against justice and humanity. Let the example of the nobles and kings be a lesson to you. Learn to savour the charms of equality and the delights of virtue; or at least be content with the advantages that fortune gives you, and leave the people some bread, work and morals. The enemies of liberty thrash about in vain to tear the bosom of their homeland; they will no more stay the course of human reason than that of the sun; cowardice shall never triumph over courage; the spirit of intrigue had better flee before the spirit of liberty. And you, legislators, remember that you are the representatives not of a privileged caste, but of the French people; do not forget that the source of order is justice; that the surest guarantor of public peace is the well-being of the citizens, and that the long convulsions that tear states apart are only the combat of prejudice against principle, egoism against the general interest, the arrogance and passions of powerful men against the rights, and the needs, of the weak.

8

ON THE TRIAL OF THE KING

3 December 1792[1]

After the overthrow of the monarchy on 10 August 1792, the question of the fate of the king was posed. The Convention was divided; Robespierre was against a trial, considering the former monarch as already condemned. After several votes, both the Girondin 'Appeal to the People' and the suspended sentence were rejected and Louis XVI was executed on 21 January 1793.

Citizens,

The Assembly has been led, without realizing it, far from the real question. There is no trial to be held here. Louis is not a defendant. You are not judges. You are not, you cannot be anything but statesmen and representatives of the nation. You have no sentence to pronounce for or against a man, but a measure of public salvation to implement, an act of national providence to perform. A dethroned king, in the Republic, is good for only two uses: either to trouble the peace of the state and threaten liberty, or to affirm both of these at the same time. Now I maintain that the character of your deliberation so far runs directly counter to that goal. In fact, what is the decision that sound policy prescribes to consolidate the nascent Republic? It is to engrave contempt for royalty deeply on people's hearts and dumbfound all the king's supporters. Thus, to present his crime to the universe as a problem, to treat his cause as an object of the most imposing, the most religious, the most difficult discussion that could occupy the representatives of the French people; to establish an immeasurable distance between the mere memory of what he was and the dignity of a citizen, amounts precisely to having found the secret of keeping him dangerous to liberty.

Louis was king, and the Republic is founded: the famous question you are considering is settled by those words alone. Louis was dethroned by his crimes; Louis denounced the French people as rebellious; to chastise it, he called on the arms of his fellow tyrants; victory and the people decided that he was the rebellious one: therefore Louis cannot be judged; either he is already condemned or the Republic is not acquitted. Proposing to put Louis on trial, in whatever way that could be done, would be to regress towards royal and constitutional despotism; it is a counter-revolutionary idea, for it means putting the revolution itself in contention. In fact, if Louis can still be put on trial, then he can be acquitted; he may be innocent; what am I saying! He is presumed to be so until he has been tried. But if Louis is acquitted, if Louis can be presumed innocent, what becomes of the revolution? If Louis is innocent, then all defenders of liberty become slanderers; the rebels were the friends of truth and defenders of oppressed innocence; all the manifestos from foreign courts are just legitimate complaints against a dominant faction. Even the detention Louis has suffered so far is an unjust vexation; the *fédérés*, the people of Paris, all the patriots of the French empire are guilty; and, pending nature's tribunal, this great trial between crime and virtue, between liberty and tyranny, is decided in favour of crime and tyranny.

Citizens, have a care; you are being misled here by false notions. You are confusing the rules of civil and statute law with the principles of the law of nations; you are confusing relations between citizens with those between a nation and an enemy conspiring against it. You are also confusing the situation of a people in revolution with that of a people whose government is soundly established. You are confusing a nation that punishes a public official while conserving the form of the government, with one that destroys the government itself. We refer to ideas familiar to us to understand an extraordinary case that functions on principles we have never applied. Thus, because we are accustomed to seeing offences we have witnessed judged according to uniform rules, we are naturally inclined to believe that under no circumstances can nations equitably punish a man who has violated their rights in any other way; and that where we do not see a jury, a bench, proceedings, we do not find justice. These very terms, when we apply them to ideas different from the ones they normally express, end by misleading us. Such is the natural dominion of habit that we regard the most arbitrary conventions, sometimes indeed the most defective institutions, as absolute measures of truth or falsehood, justice or injustice. It does not even occur to us that most are inevitably still connected with the prejudices on which despotism fed us. We have been so long stooped under its yoke that we have some difficulty in raising ourselves to the eternal principles of reason; anything that refers to the sacred source of all law seems to us to take on an illegal character, and the very order of nature seems to us a disorder. The majestic movements of a great people, the sublime fervours of virtue often appear to our timid eyes as something like an erupting volcano or the overthrow of political society; and it is certainly not the least of the troubles bothering us, this contradiction between the weakness of our morals, the depravity of our minds, and the purity of principle and energy of character demanded by the free government to which we have dared aspire.

When a nation has been forced to resort to the right of insurrection, it returns to the state of nature in relation to the tyrant. How can the tyrant invoke the social pact? He has annihilated it. The nation can still keep it, if it thinks fit, for everything concerning relations between citizens; but the effect of tyranny and insurrection is to break it entirely where the tyrant is concerned; it places them reciprocally in a state of war. Courts and legal proceedings are only for members of the same side.

It is a gross contradiction to suppose that the constitution might preside over this new order of things; that would be to assume it had itself survived. What are the laws that replace it? Those of nature, the one which is the foundation of society itself: the salvation of the people. The right to punish the tyrant and the right to dethrone him are the same thing; both include the same forms. The tyrant's trial is the insurrection; the verdict, the collapse of his power; the sentence, whatever the liberty of the people requires.

Peoples do not judge in the same way as courts of law; they do not hand down sentences, they throw thunderbolts; they do not condemn kings, they drop them back into the void; and this justice is worth just as much as that of the courts. If it is for their salvation that they take arms against their oppressors, how can they be made to adopt a way of punishing them that would pose a new danger to themselves?

We have allowed ourselves to be led into error by foreign examples that have nothing in common with us. Cromwell had Charles I tried by a judicial commission he controlled;[2] Elizabeth had Mary Queen of Scots condemned in the same way;[3] it is natural that tyrants who sacrifice their fellows, not to the people, but to their own ambition, should seek to mislead vulgar opinion with illusory forms. There is no question there of principle or liberty, but of deceit and intrigue. But the people! What other law can it follow, than justice and reason supported by its own absolute power?

In what republic was the need to punish the tyrant a legal matter? Was Tarquin called to trial?[4] What would have been said in Rome, if Romans had dared say they were his defenders? And what are we doing? We are summoning lawyers from every side to plead the cause of Louis XVI.

We are establishing as legitimate acts what any free people would have regarded as the greatest of crimes. We are ourselves inviting the citizens to baseness and corruption. We could well find ourselves one day awarding Louis's defenders civic crowns; for if they defend his cause, they may hope to make it triumph; otherwise you would be showing the universe nothing but a ridiculous charade. And we dare to use the word Republic! We invoke forms, because we have no principles; we pride ourselves on our delicacy, because we lack energy; we flaunt a false humanity, because the feeling of true humanity is foreign to us; we revere the shadow of a king, because we do not know how to respect the people; we are tender towards oppressors, because we are heartless towards the oppressed.

The trial of Louis XVI! But what is that trial, if not a call for insurrection in some tribunal or assembly? When a king has been annihilated by the people, who has the right to resuscitate him and make him a new pretext for trouble and rebellion, and whatever other effects this scheme might produce? By opening an arena for the champions of Louis XVI, you are renewing the quarrels of despotism against liberty, you are establishing the right to blaspheme against the Republic and against the people; for the right to defend the former despot carries with it the right to say anything appropriate to his cause. You awaken all the factions; you revive and encourage dormant royalism: people can take sides freely for or against. What could be more legitimate, what more natural than to repeat everywhere the maxims that his defenders will be able to profess openly at your bar and in your parliament itself! What sort of republic is it whose founders seek out adversaries for it on all sides to attack it in its cradle!

See what rapid progress this scheme has made already. Last August, all the partisans of royalty were hiding: anyone who had dared attempt an apologia for Louis XVI would have been punished as a traitor. Today they are again showing a bold front, with impunity; today the aristocracy's most deplored scribblers are confidently taking up their poisonous pens once more.

Today, the insolent writings that are the precursors to all attacks are flooding the city where you reside, all the eighty-four departments and up to the very portals of this sanctuary of liberty. Today armed men, conscripts, kept inside these walls without your knowledge and against the law, made the streets of this city resound with seditious cries demanding impunity for Louis XVI. Today Paris contains within it men brought together, you have been told, to snatch him from the nation's justice. All that remains for us to do is to throw open these premises to the athletes already flocking to solicit the honour of taking up cudgels on behalf of royalty. What am I saying! Today Louis divides the people's representatives; some speak for him, some speak against him. Two months ago, who would have suspected that there could be any question over whether he was inviolable or not? But since a member of the National Convention (citizen Pétion[5]) presented the question *whether the king could be tried* as the object of a serious deliberation preliminary to every other question, inviolability, with which the conspirators in the Constituent Assembly covered his first perjuries, has been invoked to protect his latest attacks. O crime! O shame! The parliament of the French people resounded to the panegyric of Louis XVI. We have heard the virtues and good deeds of the tyrant being praised! We barely managed to rescue the honour or the liberty of the best citizens from the injustice of a precipitate decision. What am I saying? We have seen the most atrocious calumnies against people's representatives known for their zeal for liberty[6] greeted with scandalous joy. We have seen one part of this Assembly proscribed by the other almost immediately after being denounced by stupidity and depravity combined. The tyrant's cause alone is so sacred that it cannot be discussed too freely or for too long: and why should that astonish us? This double phenomenon has a single cause. Those who take an interest in Louis or his like must thirst for the blood of those people's deputies who are demanding, for the second time, that he be punished; they can pardon only those who have softened in his favour. That plan to shackle the people by killing its defenders, has it ever been abandoned for a single moment? And all the scoundrels who are proscribing them today, calling them anarchists and agitators, will they not themselves whip up the troubles their perfidious system presages for us? If we are to believe them, the trial will last several months at least; it will last until next springtime, when the despots should be making a general attack on us. And what a career open to the conspirators! What a feast for intrigue and aristocracy!

Thus, all the partisans of tyranny can still hope that help from their allies and foreign armies will encourage the boldness of the court meant to pronounce on Louis's fate, while their gold is tempting its loyalty.

God in heaven! All the ferocious hordes of despotism are preparing to tear at the breast of our homeland once again, in the name of Louis XVI! Louis is still fighting us from the depths of his dungeon; and people doubt whether he is guilty, whether it is permitted to treat him as an enemy! They want to know what the laws are that condemn him!

The constitution is invoked in his favour. I do not intend to repeat here all the unanswerable arguments developed by those who deign to answer objections of that sort. On this matter I will just say a word for the benefit of those whom they have not convinced. The constitution forbade everything you have done. Even if he could only be punished by forced abdication, you could not pronounce sentence without having brought him to trial. You have no right at all to hold him in prison. He has the right to ask you for his release and for damages and interest. The constitution condemns you: fall at Louis XVI's feet and ask for his clemency.

Personally, I should blush to discuss these constitutional quibbles any more seriously than that; they belong on school or palace benches, or rather in the cabinets of London, Vienna and Berlin. I cannot argue at length when I am convinced that deliberation is a scandal.

This is a great cause, we have been told, and one that should be judged with wise and slow circumspection. It is you who are making it a great cause! What am I saying? It is you who are making it a cause. What do you find in it that can be called great? Is it the difficulty? No. Is it the person? From the viewpoint of liberty, there is none more vile; from that of humanity, none more guilty. Now he can only impress those more cowardly than he is himself. Is it the usefulness of the outcome? That is one more reason to hasten it. A great cause would be a popular draft law; a great cause would be that of a poor man oppressed by despotism. What is the motive for these endless delays you are urging on us? Are you afraid of hurting the people's opinion? As if the people itself feared anything other than the weakness or ambition of its representatives; as if the people were a foul herd of slaves stupidly attached to the tyrant it has proscribed, and wishing at all costs to wallow in baseness and servitude. You talk about opinion; is it not for you to direct it, to fortify it? If it wanders, if it becomes depraved, who should get the blame, if not yourselves? Are you afraid of annoying the foreign kings in league against you? Oh yes, there is no doubt at all that the way to defeat them is to seem to fear them! That the way to confound the criminal conspiracy of European despots is to bow to their accomplice! Do you fear foreign peoples? Then you still believe in the innate love of tyranny. So why do you aspire to the glory of freeing the human race? Through what contradiction do you suppose that nations which were not astonished by the proclamation of the rights of humanity will be terrified by the chastisement of one of its most cruel oppressors? Finally, we are told, you fear the gaze of posterity. Yes; posterity will be astonished, in fact, by your irresponsibility and your weakness, and our descendants will laugh at the presumption of their fathers, and at their prejudices.

We have been told that genius would be needed to go deeply into this question; I maintain that only good faith is required. It is less a question of enlightenment than of avoiding voluntary blindness. Why is it that what seems clear to us at one time seems obscure at another? Why is it that something decided easily by the good sense of the people changes into an almost insoluble problem for its delegates? Have we the right to have a will contrary to the general will and a wisdom that differs from universal reason?

I have heard defenders of the king's inviolability advancing a bold principle that I should almost have hesitated to state myself. They said that anyone who, on 10 August, had sacrificed Louis XVI would have been performing a virtuous act; but the sole basis for that opinion can only have been Louis XVI's crimes and the people's rights. Well, has a three-month interval changed his crimes or the people's rights? The reason why he was rescued at that time from public indignation was undoubtedly so that his punishment, formally ordered by the National Convention in the nation's name, would become all the more imposing to enemies of humanity: but casting new doubt on the fact of his guilt or whether he can be punished amounts to betraying a promise given to the French people. There are perhaps some people who, either to prevent the Assembly from assuming a character worthy of it, or to deprive the nations of an example that would raise minds to the level of republican principles, or for even more shameful motives, would not be sorry if a private hand were to carry out the functions of national justice. Citizens, be wary of this trap: anyone daring to give that advice would only be serving the people's enemies. Whatever happens, the punishment of Louis will now only be good if it bears the formal character of a public vengeance.

What does the contemptible figure of the last of the kings matter to the people? Representatives, what matters to it, what matters to you yourselves, is that you fulfil the duties that its confidence has imposed on you. The Republic is proclaimed; but have you given it to us? We have not yet made a single law that justifies that name; we have not yet reformed a single abuse of despotism: alter the names, and we still have the tyranny in its entirety, and on top of that factions that are viler, charlatans still more immoral, along with new ferments of troubles and civil war. The Republic! And Louis still lives! And you still place the king's person between us and liberty! By way of scruples, let us fear making ourselves criminal; let us fear that by showing too much indulgence for the culprit we may be putting ourselves in his place.

Another difficulty. To what sentence shall we condemn Louis? The death penalty is too cruel. No, says another, life is crueller still: I demand that he live. Advocates for the king, is it from pity or cruelty that you want to shield him from the penalty for his crimes?

I myself abhor the death penalty generously prescribed by your laws; and for Louis I feel neither love nor hate; I just hate his crimes. I asked for the death penalty to be abolished in the Assembly you still name Constituent; and it is no fault of mine that the highest principles of reason seemed to it to be moral and political heresies. But you, who never think of citing them in favour of all the unfortunates whose offences are less theirs than the government's, by what fluke do you now recall them to plead the cause of the greatest criminal of all? You are demanding an exception to the death penalty for the one individual who can justify it. Yes, the death penalty, in general, is a crime, and for the sole reason that, in keeping with the indestructible principles of nature, it can only be justified where it is necessary for the security of individuals or the social body. Now public security never requires it for ordinary offences, because society can always stop them by other means and make the culprit powerless to damage it. But a dethroned king in the middle of a revolution which is nothing unless consolidated by the laws, a king whose name alone calls down the scourge of war on the disturbed nation: neither prison nor exile can render his existence harmless to the public good; and this cruel exception that justice allows to ordinary laws can be imputed only to the nature of his crimes.

I utter this deadly truth with regret, but Louis must die, because the homeland has to live. Among a peaceable, free people, respected at home and abroad, you might listen to the advice being given you to be generous; but a people whose liberty is still being disputed after so many sacrifices and battles, a people in whose country the laws are still only inexorable towards the unfortunate, a people in whose country the crimes of tyranny are still subjects of dispute, such a people must want to be avenged; and the generosity for which you are being praised would resemble too much that of a society of bandits sharing out spoils.

I propose that you give an immediate ruling on Louis's fate. As for his wife, you will send her back to the courts, along with all the individuals aware of the same attacks. His son will be kept in the Temple, until such time as peace and public liberty should be established. As for Louis, I ask that the National Convention *declare him from this moment a traitor to the French nation, a criminal towards humanity*; I ask that a great example be given to the world, at the same place where, on 10 August, the generous martyrs to liberty lost their lives. I ask that this memorable event be commemorated with a monument to nourish in the hearts of peoples the sense of their rights and horror of tyrants; and in the minds of tyrants, salutary terror of the people's justice.

9

DRAFT DECLARATION OF THE RIGHTS OF MAN AND OF THE CITIZEN

24 April 1793[1]

In this speech at the Convention, Robespierre proposed a draft declaration against the Girondin draft, written by Condorcet, which sanctified property rights. The proposals he put forward here, aiming to limit property rights, were not included in the Constitution of 1793.

I will start by proposing some articles needed to complete your theory on property. Let this word alarm no one: muddy souls, who value nothing but gold, I do not mean to touch your treasures, however impure their source may be. You must know that the agrarian law[2] you have discussed at such length is just a phantom conjured up by rogues to scare imbeciles.

There was no need for a revolution, surely, to teach the universe that extreme disproportion between fortunes is the source of many ills and many crimes, but we are nevertheless convinced that equality of possessions is a chimera. Personally, I believe it is even less necessary to private happiness than to public felicity: the question is more one of making poverty honourable than of banning opulence, Fabricius's[3] cottage having nothing to envy in the palace of Crassus.[4] For myself, I would be just as happy to be one of the sons of Aristides,[5] raised in the Prytaneum[6] at the Republic's expense, as I would to be heir presumptive to Xerxes,[7] born in the filth of courts to occupy a throne decorated with the degradation of peoples, and glittering with public misery.

So let us in good faith set out the principles of the right to property; something all the more necessary since the prejudices and vices of men have sought to envelop the question in impenetrable fog.

Ask some merchant of human flesh what property is; he will tell you, pointing towards the long coffin that he calls a ship, in which he has packed and fettered men who appear to be alive: 'There are my properties; I bought them for so much a head.' Question some gentleman who has land and vassals, or who thinks the universe turned upside down because he has them no longer, and he will give you ideas on property that are more or less similar.

Interrogate the august members of the Capet dynasty;[8] they will tell you that the most sacred of all properties is unquestionably the hereditary right they have enjoyed since ancient times, to oppress, degrade and squeeze legally and monarchically the twenty-five millions of men who inhabit the territory of France, subject to their good pleasure.

In the eyes of all those people, property does not rest on any principle of morality. It excludes all notions of justice or injustice. Why does your Declaration of Rights seem to present the same error? In defining liberty, the first of mankind's assets, the most sacred of the rights it receives from nature, you said, rightly, that its limits were the rights of others: why did you not apply that principle to property, which is a social institution? As if the eternal laws of nature were less inviolable than the conventions of men. You added more and more articles to ensure the greatest liberty for the exercise of property, but said not a single word to determine its legitimate character; so that your declaration appears to be made, not for men, but for the rich, for monopolists [*accapareurs*],[9] for speculators and tyrants. I suggest that you reform these faults by including the following truths.

Article I. Property is the right every citizen has to enjoy and dispose of the portion of goods guaranteed to him by the law.

II. The right to property is limited, like all others, by the obligation to respect the rights of other people.

III. It cannot prejudice either the security, or the liberty, or the life, or the property of our fellows.

IV. Any possession or any trade that violates that principle is illicit and immoral.

You are also talking about taxation to establish the incontestable principle that it can only emanate from the will of the people or its representatives; but you are forgetting an arrangement required by the interest of humanity; you are forgetting to establish a progressive basis for taxation. Now, where public contributions are concerned, is there any principle more obviously derived from the nature of things and from eternal justice, than one that obliges the citizens to contribute to public expenditure progressively, in accordance with the size of their fortune, in other words in accordance with the advantages they draw from society?

I propose that you put it into an article conceived in these terms:

'Those citizens whose incomes do not exceed what is necessary for their subsistence should be exempted from contributing to public expenditure, others should contribute progressively in accordance with the extent of their wealth.'

The committee has also completely forgotten to quote the duties of fraternity which unite all men and all nations, and their rights to mutual assistance; it seems to have been unaware of the foundations of the eternal alliance of peoples against tyrants; one might say that your declaration had been made for a herd of human creatures parked in some corner of the globe, and not for the immense family to which nature has given the earth as its domain and abode. I propose that you fill this big lacuna with the following articles; they cannot but win you the esteem of peoples: it is true that they may have the drawback of setting you irrevocably at odds with kings. I confess that this drawback does not frighten me; nor will it frighten anyone who does not want to be reconciled with them.

Article I. The men of all countries are brothers, and different peoples should help each other to the best of their ability, like citizens of the same state.

II. He who oppresses one nation declares himself the enemy of all.

III. Those who make war on a people to arrest the progress of liberty and annihilate the rights of man should be pursued by all, not as ordinary enemies but as murderers and rebellious brigands.

IV. Kings, aristocrats, tyrants, whatever they be, are slaves in revolt against the sovereign power of the earth, which is the human race, and against the legislator of the universe, which is nature.

Declaration of the Rights of Man and of the Citizen, proposed by Maximilien Robespierre, printed by order of the National Convention

The representatives of the French people assembled in the National Convention, recognizing that human laws which do not derive from the eternal laws of justice and reason are merely attacks on humanity by ignorance or despotism; convinced that neglect or contempt of the natural rights of man are the only causes of the world's crimes and misfortunes, have resolved to set out those sacred, inalienable rights in a solemn Declaration, so that all citizens, able continuously to compare the actions of the government with the goal of every social institution, will never allow themselves to be oppressed and degraded by tyranny; so that the people has always before its eyes the foundations of its liberty and happiness; the magistrate, the rule of his duties; the legislator, the object of his mission.

Consequently, the National Convention proclaims, before the universe and under the gaze of the immortal legislator, the following Declaration of the Rights of Man and of the Citizen.

Article I. The goal of every political association is the maintenance of the natural and imprescriptible rights of man, and the development of all his faculties.

II. The principal rights of man are the right to provide for the preservation of his existence and liberty.

III. These rights belong equally to all men, whatever the differences in their physical and moral strength.

Equality of rights is established by nature: society, far from threatening it, only guarantees it against the abuse of force which renders it illusory.

IV. Liberty is the power that man has to exercise all his faculties at will. Justice is its rule, the rights of others are its borders, nature is its principle and law its safeguard.

V. The right to assemble peacefully, the right to express opinion either in print or in any other way, are such inevitable results of the principle of human liberty that the need to state them implies the presence or recent memory of despotism.

VI. Property is the right of every citizen to enjoy and dispose of the portion of goods guaranteed to him by the law.

VII. The right to property is limited, like all the others, by the obligation to respect the rights of other people.

VIII. It cannot prejudice either the security, or the liberty, or the life, or the property of our fellows.

IX. Any trade that violates that principle is essentially illicit and immoral.

X. Society is obliged to provide for the subsistence of all its members, either by procuring work for them, or by ensuring the means to exist for those who are not fit to work.

XI. The support essential to those who lack what is necessary is a debt owed by those possessing superfluous means: it is for the law to determine the way this debt should be acquitted.

XII. Citizens whose income does not exceed what is necessary for their subsistence are exempted from contributing to public expenditure. The rest should contribute progressively, according to the extent of their means.

XIII. Society should favour the development of public reason with all its strength, and make education accessible to all citizens.

XIV. The people is sovereign: the government is its product and its property, public officials are its assistants. The people may, if it wishes, change its government and revoke its representatives.

XV. The law is the free and solemn expression of the people's will.

XVI. The law is equal for all.

XVII. The law can only forbid what is damaging to society: it can only order what is useful to it.

XVIII. Any law that violates the imprescriptible rights of man is essentially unjust and tyrannical: it is not a law.

XIX. In any free state, the law above all should defend public and individual liberty against abuse of authority by those who govern.

Any institution that does not assume the people to be good, and the magistrate corruptible, is itself depraved.

XX. No portion of the people may exercise the power of the entire people; but the wish it expresses should be respected as the wish of a portion of the people, which should contribute to forming the general will.

Each section of the sovereign assembly should enjoy the right to express its will, with entire liberty; it is essentially independent of all the constituted authorities, and in charge of regulating its own policies and deliberations.

XXI. All citizens are eligible for all public functions, without distinction other than their virtues and talents, and with no qualification other than the confidence of the people.

XXII. All citizens have an equal right to contribute to the appointment of the people's representatives, and to the formation of the law.

XXIII. In order that these rights should not be illusory, and equality chimerical, society should pay a salary to public officials, and make arrangements for citizens who live by their work to attend those public assemblies to which they are summoned by law, without compromising their livelihood or that of their families.

XXIV. Every citizen must obey religiously magistrates and agents of the government, when they are the voices or executors of the law.

XXV. But any act against the liberty, security or property of a man, exercised by anyone, even in the name of the law, apart from cases determined by the law and in the forms prescribed by it, is arbitrary and null and void; respect for the law itself forbids submission to such an act, and if violence is used in its execution, it is permitted to resist it by force.

XXVI. The right to submit petitions to holders of public authority belongs to every individual. Those to whom they are addressed should give a ruling on the points raised in them, but may never forbid, restrict or condemn their submission.

XXVII. Resistance to oppression is the consequence of the other rights of man and of the citizen.

XXVIII. There is oppression of the social body, when just one of its members is oppressed.

There is oppression of every member of the social body, when the social body is oppressed.

XXIX. When the government violates the people's rights, insurrection is, for the people and each portion of the people, the most sacred of rights and the most indispensable of duties.

XXX. When the social guarantee is lacking to a citizen, he reverts to the natural right to defend all his rights for himself.

XXXI. In both these cases, subjecting resistance against oppression to legal forms is the ultimate refinement of tyranny.

XXXII. Public functions may not be considered as distinctions or as rewards, but as public duties.

XXXIII. Offences committed by people's representatives should be severely and promptly punished. No one has the right to claim to be more inviolable than other citizens.

XXXIV. The people has the right to know all the operations of its representatives; they must give it an honest account of their management, and submit to its judgement with respect.

XXXV. Men of all countries are brothers, and the different peoples should help one another to the best of their ability, like citizens of the same state.

XXXVI. He who oppresses a single nation declares himself the enemy of all.

XXXVII. Those who make war on a people to arrest the progress of liberty and annihilate the rights of man should be pursued by all, not as ordinary enemies but as murderers and rebellious brigands.

XXXVIII. Kings, aristocrats, tyrants, whatever they be, are slaves in revolt against the sovereign power of the earth, which is the human race, and against the legislator of the universe, which is nature.

10

EXTRACTS FROM 'IN DEFENCE OF THE COMMITTEE OF PUBLIC SAFETY AND AGAINST BRIEZ'

25 September 1793[1]

At the end of September 1793 the Convention was faced with an opposition. Briez, a representative of the Assembly on mission in the North, presented a report on the state of the army in the region, criticizing the Committee of Public Safety for not having taken the necessary measures. Seizing the occasion of this weakness, the opposition appointed Briez to the Committee, which it in its turn refused. Robespierre here justifies the measures taken, following which the Committee renewed its confidence in him.

[. . .]

For some time past the Committee of Public Safety has endured the war being waged on it by some members who are more envious and prejudiced than they are just. While it is busy day and night with the great interests of the homeland, people come here bringing you written denunciations, shrewdly laid out. Could it be then that the citizens you have dedicated to the most arduous tasks have lost the title of imperturbable defenders of liberty, because they accepted this burden? Are those who attack them more patriotic, because they have not received this mark of confidence? Do you maintain that those who have defended liberty and the people's rights here at the risk of their lives, amid daggers, ought to be treated like vile protectors of the aristocracy? We can stand the calumny and intrigues. But the Convention is connected to the Committee of Public Safety; your glory is bound up with the success of those you have clothed in the nation's confidence.

We are accused of doing nothing; but has our position really been considered? Eleven armies to run, the weight of all Europe to bear; everywhere traitors to expose, emissaries bribed with the gold of foreign powers to foil, disloyal administrators to supervise, to prosecute; everywhere obstacles and hindrances blocking the execution of wise measures to be smoothed out; all the tyrants to fight, the conspirators to intimidate, almost all of them from a caste once so powerful through its wealth, and still through its intrigues: such are our functions. Do you believe that without unity of action, without secrecy in its operations, without the certainty of finding support in the Convention, the government could triumph over so many obstacles and enemies? No; only the most extreme ignorance, the deepest perversity, could claim that in such circumstances a man would not be an enemy of the homeland if he made a cruel game of degrading those at the helm of affairs, of hampering their operations and slandering their conduct. Your failure to find the necessary strength of opinion would not go unpunished. I need no evidence other than the discussions that have just taken place.

The Committee of Public Safety sees betrayals in the middle of a victory. It dismisses a general, still filled with the confidence and swathed in the glitter of an apparent triumph; and its very courage is called a crime! It expels traitors, and looks over the officers who have shown most public spirit; it chooses them after consulting those people's representatives who had specific knowledge of the character of each. This operation required secrecy to be fully successful; the safety of the homeland demanded it. All the necessary measures had been taken to maintain this secrecy, even from the other armies. Well! As we waited impatiently to know the result of these measures, we were denounced to the National Convention; our work is criticized in ignorance of its motives; people want us to divulge the Republic's secrets, to give the traitors time to escape; they seek to show the new choices in an unfavourable light, undoubtedly to prevent confidence from being restored.

There is constant ranting against nobles; people say that they should be dismissed; and by a strange contradiction, when we execute that great revolutionary measure, and even do it as tactfully as possible, we are denounced. We have just sacked two nobles, to wit, one of the men of that proscribed caste, most suspect for their ancient relations with the court, and another known for his links and frequent contacts with foreign nobles, both markedly aristocratic.[2] Well! We are accused of disorganizing everything. We were told people only wanted to see real *sans-culottes* at the head of our armies. We chose those whose new exploits in the business at Bergues and Dunkirk had marked them for national recognition, who won despite Houchard, and who had displayed the greatest talent, for the Hondschoote attack should have been the end of the French army;[3] the astonishing success that honoured that army, which forced the siege of Dunkirk to be lifted, is due mainly to Jourdan;[4] he is the officer who, when the army unexpectedly found eighteen thousand men well dug in, and was surprised by a frightening artillery barrage, this Jourdan was the one who charged at the head of a battalion into the enemy camp, who passed his courage to the rest of the army, and the capture of Hondschoote was the effect of his skilful deployments and the ardour he managed to inspire.

The chief of staff being rightly regarded with suspicion, we replaced him with a man whose talents and patriotism were attested by all the commissioners; a man known for exploits that singled him out at the very time when the most odious treasons were sacrificing that army. He is called Ernould;[5] he distinguished himself in the recent business, and even sustained wounds. And they denounce us!

We made similar changes in the armies of Moselle and the Rhine; all the choices were men of the same character as those I have just described to you. And still they accuse us!

If there are any moral assumptions that could guide the government and serve as rules for legislators, we certainly followed them in these operations.

So what is the cause of this denunciation?

Ah! That day was worth more to Pitt,[6] I daresay, than three military victories. What success can he claim, really, unless he can annihilate the national government the Convention has established, divide us, make us tear ourselves apart with our own hands? And if we are seen throughout Europe as imbeciles or traitors, do you imagine the Convention that chose us will be any more respected, or indeed that people will be disposed to respect any authorities you establish later?

It is important therefore that the government take on some substance, and that you replace a Committee that has been denounced with success in your assembly. [*Unanimous cries of No! No!*]

Individuals are not at issue here; we are concerned with the homeland and principles. I tell you plainly: it is impossible, in this state of affairs, for the Committee to save the state; and if anyone disagrees, I will remind you just how treacherous and extensive is the scheme for bringing us down and dissolving us; how the foreigners and internal enemies have agents paid to execute it; I will remind you that faction is not dead; that it is conspiring from the depths of its dungeons; that the serpents of the Marais have not yet all been crushed.[7] [*Applause*]

The men who rant perpetually, here and elsewhere, against men who are at the head of government, have themselves given proof of baseness or lack of public spirit. Why then do people want to degrade us? Which of our actions is it that has brought this ignominy on us?

I know we cannot flatter ourselves that we have attained perfection; but holding up a Republic surrounded by enemies, fortifying reason in favour of liberty, destroying prejudice and nullifying individual efforts against the public interest, demand moral and physical strengths that nature has perhaps denied to those who denounce us and those we are fighting.

The Committee has a right to the hatred of kings and rogues; if you do not believe in its zeal, in the services it has rendered to the state, then break that instrument; but first consider what circumstances you are in. Those who denounce us are themselves denounced to the Committee; from being accusers today, they are going to become accused. [*Applause*] But what sort of men are they who are contesting the Committee's conduct, and who in this session have exaggerated your reversals, to aggravate their denunciations?

The first declared himself a supporter of Custine[8] and Lamarlière;[9] he was the persecutor of patriots in a major fortress, and again recently dared to advance the idea of abandoning a territory joined to the Republic, whose inhabitants, betrayed by him, are today defending themselves energetically against fanatics and the English.

The second has not yet dispelled the shame of having returned from a place he had been entrusted with defending, after giving it up to the Austrians. If such men succeed in proving that the Committee is not composed of good citizens, there is no doubt that liberty is lost; for there is no doubt either that it would not be to them that enlightened opinion would transfer its confidence, and hand over the reins of government! Let no one think that my intention here is to answer one accusation with another. I am committed to never dividing the patriots; but I do not count as patriots those who only wear the mask of patriotism, and I will expose the conduct of two or three traitors who are the artisans of discord and dissension here. [*Applause*]

So I think the homeland is lost if the government does not enjoy unlimited confidence, and if it is not composed of men who merit that confidence. I demand that the Committee of Public Safety be replaced. [*Emphatic cries of No! No!*]

[. . .] Moving on to the order of the day means opening the door to all the problems I have mentioned. The Convention cannot stay silent on that which tends to paralyse government. The explanations that have been given are inadequate: the result is that those members of the Committee of Public Safety who spoke have seemed to be defending their cause, and you have not given your verdict; that gives the advantage to the men who have slandered it, not always here, but secretly, all the more perfidiously in that they pretend to applaud in front of you when it gives its reports; for I tell you, the most distressing thing I have experienced during this discussion was the sight of Barère being applauded by the very people who have slandered all the Committee's members constantly and indiscriminately, the very people who would perhaps like to see us with a knife between our ribs. [*Applause*]

A member said that everyone ought to be able to utter his opinion on the operations of the Committee of Public Safety: I do not deny it. The functions of the Committee of Public Safety are arduous, and because of that it could never save the homeland without the Convention. Saving the homeland calls for great character, great virtues; it calls for men with the courage to propose strong measures, and who even dare to attack the conceit of individuals. [*Applause*] No doubt everyone is free to say what he thinks of the Committee in his own way; but that liberty should not go so far that a deputy who is recalled from the depths of the departments, because he is thought to have stopped serving the people well, can put himself forward and accuse the Committee. [*Applause*]

Citizens, I promised you the whole truth, I am going to tell it: In this discussion, the Convention has not shown all the energy it should have; you have heard a report on Valenciennes, whose apparent purpose was to inform you of all the circumstances around the surrender of that place, but whose real object was to indict the Committee of Public Safety. As a prize for his vague accusations, the author of that report is added to the Committee he denounces. Well! I tell you, someone who was at Valenciennes when the enemy entered it is not fit to be a member of the Committee of Public Safety. [*Loud applause*] This member will never answer the question: *Did you die?* [*Repeated applause*] If I had been at Valenciennes in those circumstances, I would never have been in a position to give you a report on the events of the siege; I would have wanted to share the fate of those brave defenders who preferred honourable death to shameful capitulation. [*Applause*] And since we need to be republican, since we need to have energy, I declare to you that I would never serve on a committee that included such a man.

That may appear harsh; but what seems harsher still to a patriot is that over the past two years, a hundred thousand men have been slaughtered through treason and through weakness: it is weakness towards traitors that is ruining us. People feel sorry for the most criminal individuals, for those who expose the homeland to enemy steel; I myself only know how to feel sorry for unfortunate virtue; I only know how to feel sorry for oppressed innocence; I only know how to feel sorry for the lot of a generous people being butchered with such villainy. [*Applause*]

I will add a word on the subject of our accusers; freedom of opinion should not serve as a pretext for a committee, which serves the homeland well, being slandered with impunity by those who were in a position to crush one of the heads of the federalist hydra, but failed to do it through excessive weakness; or by those who at this tribune dared coolly to propose that we hand Mont Blanc over to the Piedmontese. [*Applause*]

As for Billaud-Varenne's proposal, I attach no importance to it, and I think it impolitic. If the 50 million made available to the Committee could command the Convention's attention for a single moment, it would be unworthy to work for the salvation of the homeland. I maintain that one does not have to believe in probity to be suspicious of the Committee of Public Safety. [*Applause*] That the tyrants who detest us, that their paid slanderers, the journalists who serve them so well, are spreading these lies to bring us down, I can understand; but it is not for us to foresee such accusations and answer them; it is enough for me to feel in my heart the strength to defend to the death the people's cause, which is great and sublime; it is enough for me to despise all tyrants and all the scoundrels who support them. [*Applause*]

To sum up, I would say that all the explanations that have been given are inadequate. We can despise calumny; but agents of the tyrants surrounding us are watching us and gathering anything that can bring down the people's defenders; it is because of them, to ward off their impostures, that the National Convention should proclaim that it still has full confidence in the Committee of Public Safety. [*Applause*]

II

EXTRACTS FROM 'REPORT ON THE POLITICAL SITUATION OF THE REPUBLIC'

(18 November 1793/27 Brumaire Year II)[1]

While the Republican armies were succeeding in blocking the invasion forces of the coalition of foreign powers, Robespierre was charged by the Committee of Public Safety to present a report on the situation of France in which he laid out what was at stake in the revolutionary process.

Citizen people's representatives,

Today we are drawing the attention of the National Convention to the greatest interests of the homeland. We are here to place before you the situation of the Republic in relation to the various powers of the world, and in particular those peoples attached to our cause by nature and reason; but that intrigue and perfidy seek to range with our enemies.

As we emerge from the chaos into which the treasons of a criminal Court and the reign of the factions had plunged the government, the French people's legislators should determine the principles of their policy towards the friends and enemies of the Republic; they should deploy before the eyes of the universe the real character of the nation they have the glory of representing. It is time to teach the imbeciles who are unaware of it, and the perverts who pretend to doubt it, that the French Republic exists; that there is nothing precarious in the world but the triumph of crime and the endurance of despotism; it is time for our allies to show as much faith in our wisdom and luck as the tyrants bearing arms against us fear our courage and power.

The French Revolution gave the world a shock. The fervour for liberty of a great people was bound to displease the kings who surrounded it. But it was a long way from that unspoken attitude to the perilous resolution to declare war on the French people, and even further to the monstrous league of so many powers essentially divided in their interests.

To unite them, what was needed was the policy of two courts whose influence dominated all the others; to embolden them, they needed alliance with the actual king of the French, and the treasons of all the factions that flattered and threatened him by turns, in order to reign in his name, or to raise another tyrant on the wreckage of his power.

A time that was to give birth to the greatest prodigies of reason was also to be tainted by the ultimate excesses of human corruption. The crimes of tyranny accelerated the advance of liberty, and the advance of liberty multiplied the crimes of tyranny by exacerbating its fear and rage. Between the people and its enemies there was a continuous reaction, whose increasing violence achieved in a few years the work of several centuries. [. . .]

Pitt was grossly mistaken about our Revolution, like Louis XVI and the French aristocrats, misled by their contempt for the people; a contempt based solely on awareness of their own baseness. Too immoral to believe in the republican virtues, too lacking in philosophy to take a step towards the future, George's minister was behind his century; the century was rushing forward to liberty and Pitt wanted to turn it back towards barbarism and towards despotism. So the general course of events has so far disappointed his ambitious dreams; the various instruments of which he made use have been broken one after another by the people's strength; he has watched them disappear, Necker, d'Orléans, La Fayette,[2] Lameth, Dumouriez, Custine, Brissot and all the pygmies of the Gironde. So far the French people has extracted itself from the threads of his intrigues, like Hercules from a spider's web. [. . .]

After 1791, the English faction and all the enemies of liberty had seen that a republican party existed in France that would not compromise with tyranny, and that that party was the people. As partial killings, such as those of the Champ-de-Mars[3] or Nancy,[4] seemed insufficient to destroy it, they resolved to make war on it: hence the monstrous alliance of Austria and Prussia, and then the league of all the powers armed against us. It would be absurd to attribute this phenomenon mainly to the influence of the émigrés, who for years, and rather to France's advantage, wearied all the courts with their impotent clamour; it was the work of the foreigners' policy, supported by the power of the agitators then governing France.

To involve the kings in this rash enterprise, it was not enough to have tried to persuade them that, apart from a few republicans, the whole nation secretly hated the new régime and was awaiting them as liberators; it was not enough to have guaranteed the treason of all the chiefs of our government and our armies: to justify this odious enterprise to their exhausted subjects, they even had to be spared the embarrassment of declaring war on us. When they were ready, the dominant faction declared it on them. You will remember with what profound cunning it contrived to involve the natural courage of the French and the civic enthusiasm of the popular societies in the furtherance of its perfidious plans.[5] You know with what Machiavellian impudence those who left our national guards without weapons, our fortresses without munitions and our armies in the hands of traitors, were urging us to go and plant the tricolour on the far edges of the world. Those treacherous ranters insulted tyrants, only to serve them; with a single stroke of the pen, they overturned all the thrones and added Europe to the French empire: a sure way to hasten the success of our enemies' plots at the moment they were urging all governments to declare against us.

The sincere partisans of the Republic thought differently. Before breaking the fetters of the entire universe, they wanted to ensure their country's liberty; before carrying war to foreign despots, they wanted to make it on the tyrant who was betraying them; convinced moreover that a king was a poor guide to lead a people to the conquest of universal liberty, and that it is for the power of reason, not the force of arms, to propagate the principles of our glorious Revolution. [. . .][6]

The time had come when the British government, after creating so many enemies for us, had resolved to join the league openly itself; but the national will and the opposition party frustrated the ministry's plan. Brissot had war declared on it: it was declared on Holland, it was declared on Spain;[7] because we were wholly unprepared to fight these new enemies, and the Spanish fleet was ready to join the English fleet.

With what base hypocrisy did the traitors make much of alleged insults to our envoys, arranged in advance between them and the foreign powers! With what impudence did they invoke the dignity of the nation, with which they were trifling so insolently!

The cowards! They had saved the Prussian despot and his army,[8] they had fertilized Belgium with Frenchmen's purest blood; more recently they were talking about municipalizing Europe, and they drove the unhappy Belgians back into the arms of their tyrants: they had delivered our treasure, our stores, our weapons, our defenders to our enemies: sure of their support, and proud of all those crimes, the vile Dumouriez had even dared to threaten liberty in its sanctuary! . . . O homeland! What tutelary divinity managed to pull thee from the immense abyss opened to swallow thee in those days of crime and calamity when, in league with thy numberless enemies, thy ingrate children plunged their parricidal hands into thy breast and seemed to be fighting over thy scattered limbs, to deliver them all bloody to the ferocious tyrants sworn against thee; in those frightful days when virtue was proscribed, perfidy crowned, calumny triumphant; when thy ports, fleets, armies, fortresses, administrators, representatives, all had been sold to thine enemies! It was not enough to have armed the tyrants against us: they wanted to condemn us to the hatred of nations, and render Revolution hideous in the eyes of the universe. Our journalists were in the pay of foreign courts, like our ministers and a portion of our legislators. Despotism and treason presented the French people to other peoples as an ephemeral and contemptible faction, the cradle of the republic as a den of crime; august liberty was travestied as a vile prostitute. For the summit of perfidy, the traitors tried to push patriotism itself into unconsidered actions, and themselves prepared the substance of their calumnies: covered in all the crimes, they accused virtue of them and flung it into dungeons, and charged with their own extravagance the friends of liberty who were its avengers or victims. Through the good offices of the coalition of powerful and corrupt men, which placed in perfidious hands all the levers of government, and at the same time all the wealth, all the trumpets of renown and all the channels of opinion, the French Republic no longer had a single defender in Europe, and captive truth could find no way to cross the frontiers of France or the walls of Paris. [. . .]

Nevertheless the French people, alone in the universe, was fighting for the common cause. What became of you, you peoples allied to France? Were you only the allies of the king, and not the nation? Americans, was it the crowned automaton named Louis XVI who helped you to throw off the yoke of your oppressors, or was it our arms and our armies? Was it the wealth of a despicable court that supplied you, or was it the tributes of the French people and the products of our heaven-favoured soil? No, citizens, our allies have not abjured the sentiments they owe us: but if they have not detached themselves from our cause, if they have not ranged themselves with our enemies, it is no fault of the faction that tyrannized us. [. . .]

It will suffice to inform you of the bizarre stratagem that the Austrians tried recently. Just as I had finished this report, the Committee of Public Safety received the following note, handed to the chancery in Basle:

'It was on the 18th of October that the question of the invasion of Neufchâtel was debated in the Committee of Public Safety. The discussion was very animated: it lasted until two hours after midnight. Only one member of the minority opposed it. The business was only suspended because Saint-Just, who is its rapporteur, left for Alsace: but it is now widely known that the invasion of Neufchâtel has been decided by the committee.'

It is worth pointing out to you that there has never been any mention of Neufchâtel in the Committee of Public Safety. [. . .]

Whatever the result of this command plan may be, it can only be favourable to our cause; and if it happened that some genius inimical to humanity pushed the government of some neutral countries into the party of our common enemies, he would be betraying the people he ruled without serving the tyrants. At least we would be stronger against him for his baseness and our decency; for justice is a large part of power.

But it is important from now on to take in the whole map of Europe in a single view; what we need here is sight of the political world agitating around us and because of us.

From the moment a plan for a league against France was formed, people thought of involving the different powers with a proposal for dividing up this beautiful country. This plan is today proven, not only by the events, but by authentic documents. At the time when the Committee of Public Safety was formed, a plan of attack and dismemberment of France, drafted by the British cabinet, was communicated to the members who then comprised it.[9] Little attention was paid to it at the time, because it seemed very unlikely and because distrust of confidences of that sort is quite natural; since that time, though, the facts have verified it every day.

England had not neglected itself in the proposed division: Dunkirk, Toulon, the colonies, not to mention the chance of the crown for the Duke of York, which was not renounced, but those portions that were to form the share of other powers were sacrificed. There was no difficulty in bringing into the league the Stadtholder of Holland[10] who, as we know, is not so much the prince of the Batavians as the subject of his wife, and consequently of the Berlin court.

As for the political phenomenon of the king of Prussia's alliance with the head of the House of Austria, we have already explained it. Just as two brigands who are fighting over the spoils of some traveller they have murdered will forget their differences to rush together at a new quarry, so the Viennese monarch and the one in Berlin suspended their former differences to fall on France and devour the nascent Republic. However, the apparent conjunction of those two powers masks a real division.

Austria could well be the dupe here of the Prussian cabinet and its other allies.

The House of Austria, exhausted by the extravagances of Joseph II and Leopold,[11] long since poorly conducted by the standards of Charles V, Philip II and Maria-Theresa's[12] old ministers; Austria, today governed by the whims and the ignorance of a court of children, is expiring in the French Hainault and in Belgium. If through our own imprudence we do not help it ourselves, these last efforts against France can be regarded as the convulsions of its death agony. The empress of Russia[13] and the king of Prussia have already divided Poland without it,[14] and have presented it, as full compensation, with the conquests it might make in France with their help; in other words Lorraine, Alsace and French Flanders. England is encouraging its folly, to ruin us, while staying out of sight itself. It is trying to conserve its own forces at the expense of its ally, and advancing towards its particular goal while leaving Austria, as far as possible, to carry the whole burden of the war. On another side, the Roussillon, French Navarre and the departments bordering on Spain have been promised to his Catholic majesty.

There is no one who has not been led astray, down to the little Sardinian king with the hope that he might one day become king of the Dauphiné, Provence and the lands neighbouring his former States.

What could be offered to the powers in Italy, which cannot survive the ruin of France? Nothing. For a long time they resisted the league's solicitations; but they gave way to intrigue, or rather to the orders of the English ministry, which threatened them with fleets from England. The territory of Genoa[15] was the scene of a crime of which the history of England alone can give an example. Ships of that nation, together with French ships handed over by the Toulon traitors, entered the port of Genoa; immediately the scoundrels aboard them, English and rebel Frenchmen, seized the Republic's vessels that were in the port under the protection of the law of nations; and all the Frenchmen found in them were butchered. How cowardly it is, that Genoese senate, for not dying to a man to prevent or avenge this outrage, and for managing to betray its own honour, the Genoese people and the whole of humanity at the same time!

Venice, more powerful and also more political, has maintained a neutrality in keeping with its interests. Florence, of all the states in Italy the one to which the triumph of our enemies would be most fatal, has finally been subjugated by them and dragged against its will to its ruin. So despotism weighs down even on its accomplices, and tyrants armed against the Republic are the enemies of their own allies. In general, the Italian powers are perhaps more deserving of France's pity than her anger: England recruited them as it recruits its sailors; it press-ganged the peoples of Italy. The most culpable of the princes of that country is the king of Naples, who showed himself worthy of his Bourbon blood by embracing their cause. One day we may quote you on this subject a letter written in his own hand to his cousin the Catholic, which will serve at least to prove to you that terror is in no way foreign to the hearts of the kings allied against us. The pope is not worth the honour of a mention.

England also had the effrontery to threaten Denmark with its squadrons, to force it to comply with the league; but Denmark, ruled by an astute minister,[16] repulsed its insolent demands with dignity.

The resolution taken by the King of Sweden, Gustav III, to become generalissimo of the allied kings, can only be attributed to madness. The history of human idiocies offers nothing to compare with the delirium of that modern Agamemnon,[17] who exhausted his states and left his crown at the mercy of his enemies, to come to Paris and shore up the king of France.

The regent,[18] more wisely, paid closer attention to the interests of his country and its people; he withdrew into the terms of neutrality.

Of all the rogues decorated with the name of king, emperor, minister or politician, people insist, and are not far from believing it, that the most adroit is Catherine of Russia, or rather her ministers; for one should be suspicious of these far-off imperial reputations, prestige created by policy. The truth is that under the old empress, as under all women who hold the sceptre, it is men who govern. For the rest, the policy of Russia is imperiously determined by the very nature of things. That country combines the ferocity of savage hordes with the vices of civilized peoples. The rulers of Russia have great power and great wealth: they have the taste, the ideas, the ambition for the luxury and arts of Europe, and they reign in a climate of iron; they feel the need to be served and flattered by

Athenians, and they have Tartars for subjects: these contrasts in their situation have inevitably turned their ambition towards trade, the food of luxury and the arts, and towards conquest of the fertile lands that border them to the West and South. The Petersburg court wants to emigrate from the sad countries it inhabits to European Turkey and Poland, just as our Jesuits and aristocrats emigrated to Russia from the gentle climates of France.

She contributed greatly to the formation of the league of kings who are making war on us, and she alone profits from it. While the powers that rival her own are coming to break themselves on the rock of the French Republic, the empress of Russia is conserving her forces and building up her means; she lets her gaze wander, with secret joy, on one side over the vast territories subject to Ottoman rule, on the other over Poland and Germany: everywhere she imagines easy usurpations or rapid conquests: she believes the moment is near when she can make the law in Europe, at least she will be able to in Prussia and Austria; and in the partitioning of peoples to which she admitted those two henchmen of her august banditries, who can prevent her from taking the lion's share with impunity?

You have before your eyes Europe's record and your own, and you can already extract a major conclusion from it: that the universe has an interest in our conservation. Let us suppose France was annihilated or dismembered: the political world would crumble. Remove that powerful and necessary ally that used to guarantee the independence of mediocre states from big despots, and Europe as a whole is enslaved. The small Germanic princes, the reputedly free cities of Germany are swallowed up by the ambitious houses of Austria and Brandenburg;[19] Sweden and Denmark sooner or later fall prey to their powerful neighbours; the Turk is pushed back across the Bosphorus and erased from the list of European powers; Venice loses its wealth, its trade and its respect; Tuscany, its existence; Genoa is erased; Italy becomes the mere plaything of the despots surrounding it; Switzerland is reduced to misery, never again to recover the energy given to it by its ancient poverty; the descendants of William Tell would succumb to the efforts of tyrannies humiliated and vanquished by their ancestors. How could they dare even to invoke the virtues of their forefathers and the sacred name of liberty, if the French Republic had been destroyed before their eyes? What would they mean, if they had contributed to its ruin? And you, brave Americans, whose liberty, established by our blood, was also guaranteed by our alliance: what would be your destiny if we no longer existed? You would fall back under the shameful yoke of your former masters: the glory of our common exploits would be sullied; the titles of liberty, the declaration of the rights of humanity would be annihilated in the two worlds. [. . .]

So if the very policy of governments must dread the fall of the French Republic, what would be the attitude of philosophy and humanity? Liberty perishes in France; all nature is veiled in a funeral shroud, and human reason retreats to the abysses of ignorance and barbarity. Europe would fall prey to two or three brigands, who would avenge humanity only by making war on each other, and the fiercest of whom, by crushing its rivals, would take us back to the reign of Huns[20] and Tartars.[21] After so great an example, and so many wasted prodigies, who would ever again dare declare war on tyranny? Despotism, like a shoreless sea, would spread across the surface of the globe; soon it would cover the heights of the political world where the ark containing the charters of humanity is kept; the earth would become merely the heritage of crime; and the blasphemy uttered by the second Brutus,[22] more than justified by the impotence of our generous efforts, would become the cry of all magnanimous hearts: O Virtue, they might say, thou art then but a vain name!

Oh! Which of us does not feel all his faculties enlarged, which of us does not feel raised above humanity itself, on reflecting that we are not fighting just for one people, but for the universe; for the men who are alive today, but also for all those who will exist? Would to heaven that these salutary truths, instead of being shut inside these narrow confines, could sound at once in the ears of all peoples! At that same moment, the torches of war would be extinguished, the advantages of imposture would disappear, the fetters of the universe would be broken, the wellsprings of public calamity dried up, all peoples would become a single people of brothers, and you would have as many friends as there are men on earth. You can at least proclaim them in a way slower to establish truth. That manifesto of reason, that solemn proclamation of your principles, will be well worth the cowardly and stupid diatribes that the insolence of the vilest tyrants dares to publish against you.

Besides, should even the whole of Europe declare against you, you are stronger than Europe. The French Republic is invincible, like reason; it is immortal, like truth. When liberty has made such a conquest as France, no human power can drive it out. Tyrants, lavish your treasure, assemble your satellites, and you will hasten your ruin. Your reverses attest it; your successes even more. One port[23] and two or three fortresses bought with your gold; so that is the worthy outcome of the efforts of all those kings, helped over five years by the chiefs of our armies and by our government itself! Learn that a people you could not vanquish with such means is an invincible people. [. . .]

Force can overthrow a throne; only wisdom can found a Republic. Unravel the endless schemes of our enemies; be revolutionary and political; be terrible to the wicked and helpful to the unfortunate; avoid both cruel moderation and the systematic exaggeration of false patriots: be worthy of the people you represent; the people hates all excesses: it does not want to be deceived, or protected, it wants to be defended and honoured.

Carry illumination into the dens of these modern Cacuses[24] where they share the spoils of the people while conspiring against its liberty. Suffocate them in their lairs, and punish at last the most odious of all crimes, that of dressing up counter-revolution in the sacred emblems of patriotism, to assassinate liberty with its own weapons.

The period in which you are is the one destined to try republican virtue most sorely. At the end of that campaign, the infamous London ministry can see the league almost ruined by its crazed efforts, the arms of England dishonoured, its fortune shaken, and liberty ensured by the vigorous character you have displayed: within, it can hear the cries of the English themselves, ready to call it to account for its crimes. In its fright, it has set back until January the opening of this parliament whose approach terrifies it. It will use the time to launch the latest attacks it is plotting against you, to make up for the inability to vanquish you. All the indications, all the news, all the documents seized for some time past, refer to this project. Corrupt those people's representatives who can be corrupted, slander or murder those they cannot corrupt, and in the end achieve the dissolution of national representation, that is the objective of all the manoeuvres we are witnessing, all the patriotically counter-revolutionary means that perfidy is lavishing to whip up a riot in Paris and overthrow the entire Republic.

Representatives of the French people, be aware of your strength and dignity. You can feel a legitimate pride. Congratulate yourselves not only on having annihilated royalty and punished kings, overthrown the culpable idols to whom the world had grovelled; but above all on having astonished it with an act of justice of which it had never seen the like, by running the blade of the law across the criminal heads that rose among you, and on having so far crushed the factions with the weight of the national will!

Whatever the personal fate that awaits you, your triumph is assured. For the founders of liberty, is not death itself a triumph? Everything dies, both the heroes of humanity and the tyrants who oppress it: but under different conditions. [. . .]

One of our most sacred duties was to make you respected here and abroad. Today we have tried to give you a faithful picture of your political situation and to give Europe a high opinion of your principles. This discussion also has the specific object of exposing the plots of your enemies to turn your allies against you, especially the Swiss Cantons and the United States of America. With this in mind, we propose the following decree:

The National Convention, wishing to make clear to the universe the principles that guide it and that should govern relations between all political societies; wishing at the same time to confound the perfidious manoeuvres employed by its enemies to alarm those faithful allies of the French nation, the Swiss Cantons and the United States of America, as to its intentions;

Decrees the following:

Article I – The National Convention declares, in the name of the French people, that the firm resolve of the Republic is to be terrible to its enemies, generous to its allies, just to all peoples.

II – The treaties that bind the French people to the United States of America and the Swiss Cantons will be faithfully observed [. . .]

12

RESPONSE OF THE NATIONAL CONVENTION TO THE MANIFESTOS OF THE KINGS ALLIED AGAINST THE REPUBLIC

5 December 1793/15 Frimaire Year II[1]

On 29 Brumaire (19 November 1793) news emerged that Pitt had published a manifesto that he had sent to all the coalition powers. Robespierre was charged by the Committee of Public Safety to draft a counter-manifesto which served as the Republic's response to the coalition of monarchs.

Citizen people's representatives,

The kings allied against the Republic are making war on us with armies, intrigues and libels. We oppose their armies with braver armies; their intrigues, with vigilance and the terror of national justice; their libels, with truth.

Always busy repairing the threads of their deadly plots as soon as they are broken by the hand of patriotism; always skilled at turning the weapons of liberty against liberty itself, the emissaries of France's enemies are today working to overturn the Republic with republicanism, and reignite civil war with philosophy. This great system of subversion and hypocrisy coincides marvellously with a perfidious plan of defamation against the National Convention and the Nation itself. While perfidy or imprudence sometimes weakened the energy of revolutionary measures required for the salvation of the homeland, sometimes left them uncompleted, sometimes maliciously exaggerated them or applied them wrongly; while amid these difficulties the agents of foreign powers, putting all motives to work, distracted our attention from the real dangers and pressing needs of the Republic to fix it entirely on religious ideas; while they sought to substitute a fresh revolution for the political revolution, to mislead public reason and divert the energy of patriotism; while the same men openly attacked all religions, and secretly encouraged fanaticism; all the while making the whole of France resound with their crazed rantings, even daring to misuse the name of the National Convention to justify the calculated nonsense of the aristocracy disguised with the cloak of madness; the enemies of France were bargaining anew over your ports, your generals, your armies; comforting terrified federalism, scheming in foreign countries to make their peoples your enemies; arousing the priests of all nations against you; setting the authority of religious opinions up against the natural ascendancy of your moral and political principles; and the manifestos of all governments were denouncing us to the universe as a people of lunatics and atheists. It is for the National Convention to intervene between the fanaticism they are reviving and the patriotism they want to mislead, and to rally all the citizens to the principles of liberty, reason and justice. Legislators who love the homeland, and have the courage to save it, should not behave like reeds incessantly shaken by the breath of foreign factions. Part of the duty of the Committee of Public Safety is to expose them for you, and suggest the measures needed to stifle them; no doubt it will do so. Meanwhile, it has charged me with submitting a draft address to you, whose purpose is to confound the cowardly frauds of the tyrants in league against the Republic, and expose their hideous hypocrisy to the gaze of the Universe. In this combat between tyranny and liberty, we have so many advantages that it would be folly on our part to shirk it; and since the oppressors of the human race have the temerity to want to plead their cause before it, let us hasten to follow them into that formidable court, to accelerate the inevitable judgement that awaits them.

REPLY FROM THE NATIONAL CONVENTION, PROPOSED BY ROBESPIERRE

Will the National Convention reply to the manifestos of tyrants allied against the French Republic? It is natural to scorn them, but it would be useful to confound them; it is right to punish them.

A manifesto against liberty by despotism! What a bizarre phenomenon! How did France's enemies dare to make men the arbiters between them and us? Why did they not fear that the subject of the argument might revive the memory of their crimes and hasten their ruin?

Of what do they accuse us? Of their own heinous crimes.

They accuse us of rebellion. Slaves in revolt against the sovereignty of peoples, do you not know that this blasphemy can only be justified by victory? See then the scaffold of the last of our tyrants; see the French people armed and ready to punish his kind: that is our answer.

The kings accuse the French people of immorality! Peoples of the world, lend an attentive ear to the lessons of those upright preceptors of the human race. The morality of kings, God in heaven! Peoples, celebrate the good faith of Tiberius[2] and the candour of Louis XVI; admire the commonsense of Claudius,[3] the wisdom of George;[4] praise the temperance and justice of William and Leopold; exalt the chastity of Messalina,[5] the conjugal fidelity of Catherine, the modesty of Antoinette;[6] commend the invincible horror felt by all despots past, present and future for usurpation and tyranny; their tender concern for oppressed innocence; their religious respect for the rights of humanity.

They call us irreligious: they proclaim that we have declared war on Divinity itself. How edifying is the pity of tyrants, and how agreeable to heaven must be the virtues that glitter in courts, and the benefits they spread over the earth! What god are they talking about? Do they know any, other than pride, debauchery and all the vices? They say they are images of the Divinity . . . is that to make people hate it? They say their authority is its work. No: God created tigers; but kings are the masterpieces of human corruption. When they call on heaven, it is to usurp the earth; when they speak to us of divinity, it is to put themselves in its place; they send on to it the poor man's prayers and the groans of the unfortunate; but they are themselves the gods of the rich, of oppressors and murderers of the people. Honouring the Divinity and punishing kings are the same thing. And what people ever offered purer worship than ours to the great Being under whose auspices we proclaimed the immutable principles of every human society? The laws of eternal justice used to be called, disdainfully, the dreams of well-meaning people; we have turned them into imposing realities. Morality used to be in philosophers' books; we have put it in the government of nations. The death sentence pronounced on tyrants by nature slumbered forgotten in the dejected hearts of timid mortals; we have put it into effect. The world used to belong to a few tyrants' lineages, as the deserts of Africa belong to tigers and serpents; we have restored it to the human race.

Peoples, if you lack the strength to take back your share of this common heritage, if you cannot find a way to make the most of the rights we have returned to you, refrain at least from violating our rights or slandering our courage.

The French are not afflicted with a mania for rendering any nation happy and free against its will. All the kings could have vegetated or died unpunished on their blood-spattered thrones, if they had been able to respect the French people's independence: we want only to enlighten you on their insolent calumnies.

Your masters tell you that the French nation has proscribed all religions, that it has substituted worship of a few men for that of the Divinity; they depict us to you as an idolatrous or insane nation. They are lying: the French people and its representatives respect the freedom of all religions, and proscribe none of them. They honour the virtue of humanity's martyrs, without infatuation or idolatry; they abhor intolerance and persecution, whatever the pretext that covers them. They condemn the eccentricities of philosophism, as they do the follies of superstition and the crimes of fanaticism. Your tyrants blame us for a few irregularities, inseparable from the tempestuous movements of a great Revolution; they attribute to us the effects of their own intrigues and the attacks of their emissaries. Everything wise and sublime that the French Revolution has produced is the work of the people; everything of a different character belongs to our enemies.

All rational and magnanimous men are on the Republic's side; all perfidious and depraved creatures are of your tyrants' faction. Do we slander the star that animates nature because thin clouds slide across its shining disc? Does august Liberty lose her divine charms because vile agents of tyranny seek to profane her? Your misfortunes and ours are the crimes of the common enemies of humanity. Is that a reason for you to hate us? No; it is a reason to punish them.

The cowards dare to denounce the founders of the French Republic to you. Modern Tarquins[7] have dared to claim that the Roman senate was an assembly of brigands; even Porsena's[8] lackeys called Scaevola[9] mad. Following the manifestos of Xerxes,[10] Aristides[11] looted the treasury of Greece. Loaded down with spoils, hands stained with Roman blood, Octavian and Antony[12] ordered the whole earth to believe them alone clement, just and virtuous.

Tiberius and Sejanus[13] saw in Brutus and Cassius[14] only men of blood, and even rogues.

Frenchmen, men of all countries, it is you who are being offended when liberty is insulted, in the persons of your representatives or defenders. Several members of the Convention have been reproached for weaknesses; and others, for crimes.

Well! What has the French people got in common with all that? What has the national representation in common with it, if it is not the strength it imparts to the weak and the pain it inflicts on the guilty? All the armies of the European tyrants repelled, despite five years of betrayal, conspiracy and internal discord; the scaffold for disloyal representatives raised alongside that of the last of our tyrants; the immortal tablets on which the hand of the people's representatives engraved, amid storms and tempests, the social pact of the French; all men equal before the law, all great culprits trembling before justice; unsupported innocence, astonished to find sanctuary at last in the courts of law; love for the homeland triumphant over slavish vices, over the perfidy of our enemies; the people, energetic and wise, formidable and just, rallying to the voice of reason and learning to recognize its enemies, even through the mask of patriotism; the French people rushing to arm itself in defence of the magnificent product of its courage and virtue; that is the expiation we offer the world, both for our own errors and for the crimes of our enemies.

If need be, we can offer it other qualifications; our blood has been shed for the homeland too. The National Convention can show the friends and enemies of France honourable scars and glorious disfigurements. Here, in its view, two illustrious opponents of tyranny fell to the blows of a parricidal faction; there, a worthy emulator of their republican virtue, trapped in a besieged town, formed the brave and generous resolution to make his way, with a few companions, through the enemy hosts; that noble victim of an odious betrayal fell into the hands of Austrian satellites, and is now paying the penalty, in lengthy torment, for his sublime devotion to the cause of liberty.[15] Other representatives penetrate right through the rebel areas of the Midi, barely escaping the traitors' fury, save the French army given up by its perfidious chiefs, and turn terror and flight back on the satellites of Austrian, Spanish and Piedmontese tyrants: in that execrable town, a disgrace to the French name, Baille and Beauvais,[16] sick of tyranny's insults, died for the homeland and its holy laws. Before the walls of that sacrilegious city,

Gasparin,[17] leading the thunderbolt that was to punish it, Gasparin, inflaming our warriors' republican valour, died victim of his own courage and the villainy of our most despicable enemy. The North and South, the Alps and Pyrenees, the Rhône and the Scheldt, the Rhine and the Loire, the Moselle and the Sambre, have seen our republican battalions rally to the voice of the people's representatives behind the banners of liberty and victory: some have perished, the rest have triumphed.

The entire Convention has faced death and braved the fury of all tyrants.

Illustrious defenders of the cause of kings, princes, ministers, generals, courtiers, tell us about your civic virtues: remind us of the important services you have rendered humanity: tell us about the fortresses conquered with the force of your guineas; boast to us of the talent of your emissaries and the alacrity with which your soldiers flee the Republic's defenders; boast to us of your noble contempt for the law of peoples and for humanity; our prisoners butchered in cold blood, our women mutilated by your janissaries. Infants massacred in their mothers' arms . . . the Austrian tiger's murderous fangs tearing at their palpitating limbs: boast of your exploits in America, at Genoa and Toulon; boast above all of your supreme skill in the arts of poisoning and murder. Tyrants, behold your virtues.

Sublime parliament of Great Britain, tell us about your heroes. You have an opposition party. In your country patriotism opposes; therefore despotism triumphs; the minority opposes; therefore the majority is corrupt. Insolent and vile people; your so-called representation is venal in your own eyes and by your own admission. You quote approvingly their favourite maxim: that the talents of your members are an object of commerce, like wool from your sheep or steel from your factories . . . And you dare to speak of morality and liberty!

So what is that strange privilege of uttering endless and shameless rubbish, which the stupid patience of peoples seems to grant tyrants? What! Those little men whose chief merit consists in knowing the price list of British consciences, who work hard to transplant the vices and corruption of their country to France; who make war, not with weapons, but with crimes, have the effrontery to accuse the National Convention of corruption, and insult the virtues of the French people!

Generous people, we swear by your very existence that you will be avenged. Before making war on ourselves we will exterminate all our enemies; the house of Austria will perish rather than France; London will be free before Paris is re-enslaved. The destinies of the Republic and the tyrants of the earth have been weighed in the eternal balance; and the tyrants have been found lighter. Frenchmen, let us forget our quarrels and march on the tyrants; let us subdue them, you with your weapons and we with our laws.

Let the traitors tremble! Let the last cowardly emissary of our enemies disappear! Let patriotism triumph, and innocence take comfort! Frenchmen, fight: your cause is holy, your courage invincible; your representatives know how to die; they can do more than that: they know how to vanquish.

13

ON THE PRINCIPLES OF REVOLUTIONARY GOVERNMENT

25 December 1793/5 Nivôse Year II[1]

A month after the passage of Billaud-Varenne's decree,[2] *Robespierre defended the necessity of the Terror. It was a response to the 'Indulgents' and to Camille Desmoulins and his newspaper* Le Vieux Cordelier *in particular, who had voiced criticism of the Terror.*

Citizen people's representatives,

Successes send weak souls to sleep; they spur strong souls on. Let us leave it to Europe and history to praise the miracles of Toulon,[3] while we prepare new triumphs for liberty.

The Republic's defenders adopt Caesar's maxim: they believe nothing has been done so long as something remains to be done. We still face enough dangers to occupy all our zeal.

Vanquishing Englishmen and traitors is something easy enough for the valour of our republican soldiers; there is an enterprise that is no less important and more difficult: to confound through unwavering energy the eternal intrigues of all the enemies of our liberty, and ensure triumph for the principles on which public prosperity should be based.

Such are the first duties you have imposed on your Committee of Public Safety.

We are going to start by developing the principles and the necessity of revolutionary government; then we will show the cause that tends to paralyse it at birth.

The theory of revolutionary government is as new as the revolution which brought it into being. It should not be sought in the books of political writers, who did not foresee that revolution, nor in the laws of tyrants who, satisfied with abusing their power, are not much concerned with its legitimacy; and to the aristocracy that word is only a subject of terror or slanderous text; to tyrants, a mere scandal; to many other people, just an enigma; it needs to be explained to all, so that good citizens at least will rally to the principles of the public interest.

The function of government is to direct the moral and physical forces of the nation towards the goal of its appointing.

The goal of constitutional government is to preserve the Republic; that of revolutionary government is to found it.

Revolution is the war of liberty against its enemies; the constitution is the system of liberty victorious and at peace.

Revolutionary government needs extraordinary activity, precisely because it is at war. It is subject to less uniform and less rigorous rules, because the circumstances in which it exists are stormy and shifting, and above all because it is continually forced to deploy new resources rapidly, to confront new and pressing dangers.

Constitutional government is concerned principally with civil liberty, and revolutionary government, with public liberty. Under the constitutional system, it almost suffices to protect individuals against abuse of public power; under the revolutionary system, public power itself is obliged to defend itself against all the factions attacking it.

Revolutionary government owes good citizens full national protection; to enemies of the people it owes nothing but death.

These notions suffice to explain the origin and nature of the laws we call revolutionary. Those who call them arbitrary or tyrannical are stupid or perverse sophists seeking to confuse opposites: they want to apply the same system to peace and war, health and sickness; or rather they only want the resurrection of tyranny and the death of the homeland. If they invoke the literal execution of constitutional adages, it is just to violate them with impunity. They are cowardly assassins who, to cut the Republic's throat in its cradle without risk, try hard to muzzle it with vague maxims from which they are practised at extricating themselves.

The constitutional vessel was not built to stay in dry dock for ever; but should it have been launched in mid-tempest, into unfavourable winds? That was wanted by the tyrants and slaves who had opposed its construction; but the French people has ordered you to wait for calmer conditions. Its unanimous wishes, instantly drowning the clamour from the aristocracy and federalism, commanded you to deliver it first from all its enemies.

Temples to the gods are not meant to provide sanctuary for the sacrilegious who come to profane them; nor is the constitution supposed to protect the plots of tyrants who seek to destroy it.

If revolutionary government should be more active in its working and freer in its movements than ordinary government, does that make it less just and less legitimate? No. It is supported by the holiest of all laws: the salvation of the people; by the most indisputable of all entitlements: necessity.

It has its rules too, all drawn from justice and public order. It has nothing in common with anarchy or disorder; its purpose on the contrary is to suppress them, to introduce and consolidate the rule of law. It has nothing in common with arbitrary rule; it should not be guided by individual passions, but by the public interest.

It should come close to ordinary and general principles in all cases where they can be applied rigorously without compromising public liberty. The measure of its strength should be the boldness or perfidy of the conspirators. The more terrible it is towards the wicked, the more favourably it should treat the good. The more circumstances impose necessary rigour on it, the more it should abstain from measures that pointlessly interfere with liberty, and that jostle private interests without any public advantage.

It has to sail between two dangerous rocks, weakness and temerity, moderantism and excess;[4] moderantism, which is to moderation as impotence is to chastity, and excess, which resembles energy as dropsy resembles health.

The tyrants have sought constantly to make us retreat into servitude by the paths of moderantism; and sometimes they have also tried to drive us to the opposite extreme. Both extremes end at the same point. Whether overshot or undershot, the target is missed in both cases. Nothing resembles the apostle of federalism more closely than the untimely preacher of the single universal Republic. The friend of kings and the public prosecutor of the human race understand one another quite well.[5] The scapular-wearing fanatic and the fanatic preaching atheism have many similarities. Democratic barons are the brothers of the Koblenz[6] marquises; and sometimes red bonnets are closer to red high heels than one might think.

But here government needs to be extremely circumspect, for the enemies of liberty are looking to turn against it not only its faults, but also its wisest measures. Is the government coming down on what is called exaggeration? They seek to revive moderantism and aristocracy. If it turns its attention to those two monsters, they promote exaggeration with all their might. It is dangerous to leave them the means to mislead the zeal of good citizens; it is more dangerous still to discourage and persecute the good citizens they have deceived. Through one of these abuses, the republic would be in danger of expiring in a convulsive movement; through the other, it would infallibly pine away.

So what should be done? Hunt down the culpable inventors of perfidious schemes; protect patriotism, even in its errors; enlighten patriots; and constantly raise the people to the level of its rights and destiny.

If you do not adopt this rule, you lose everything.

If we had to choose between an excess of patriotic fervour and the total absence of civic spirit, or the stagnation of moderantism, there would be no hesitation. A vigorous body, tormented by an excess of sap, leaves more resources than a corpse.

Above all we must be careful not to kill patriotism by trying to cure it.

Patriotism is ardent by its nature. Who can love the homeland coldly? It is the gift particularly of simple men, not much given to calculating the political consequences of a civic step from its motive. Where is the patriot, even enlightened, who has never been deceived? Yes! If it is accepted that there are moderates and cowards of good faith, why should there not be patriots of good faith, who are sometimes carried away by a praiseworthy sentiment to go too far? So if we were to regard as criminals those in the revolutionary movement who might have strayed beyond the exact line drawn by prudence, we would be including in a common proscription, along with the bad citizens, all the natural friends of liberty, your own friends and the best supporters of the Republic. The adroit emissaries of tyranny, after having deceived them, would themselves then become their accusers and perhaps their judges too.

What then will disentangle all these nuances? What will trace the line of demarcation between all the contradictory excesses? Love of the homeland and truth. Kings and knaves will still be seeking to erase it; they want nothing to do with reason or with truth.

By sketching the duties of revolutionary government, we have marked the pitfalls that threaten it. The greater its power, the more free and rapid its action, the more it should be directed by good faith. On the day it falls into impure or perfidious hands, liberty will be lost; its very name will become a pretext and excuse for counter-revolution; its energy will become that of a violent poison.

The confidence of the French people is attached to the character the National Convention has shown, rather than to the institution itself.

In placing all the power in your hands, it expected your government to be beneficent to patriots, as well as formidable to enemies of the homeland. It has given you the duty to deploy all the courage and the policy needed to crush them, and above all, at the same time, to maintain the unity you need among yourselves to fulfil your great destinies.

The foundation of the French Republic is not a game for children. It cannot be the work of whim or insouciance, nor the fortuitous outcome of the clash between all the individual claims and all the revolutionary elements. Wisdom, as much as power, presided over the creation of the universe. By imposing on members drawn from among you the formidable task of watching ceaselessly over the destiny of the homeland, you have imposed the obligation on yourselves to support them with your strength and confidence. If the revolutionary government is not seconded by the energy, enlightenment, patriotism and benevolence of all the people's representatives, how can it have the strength to respond proportionately to the efforts of Europe which is attacking it, and to all the enemies of liberty pressing in on it from all sides?

Woe betide us if we open our souls to the treacherous insinuations of our enemies, who can vanquish us only by dividing us! Woe betide us if we break the bundle apart, instead of binding it; if private interests, if offended vanity be heard instead of the homeland and the truth!

Let us raise our souls to the height of republican virtues and examples from antiquity. Themistocles[7] had more genius than the Lacedaemonian general commanding the Greek fleet: however, when the general answered a much-needed piece of advice meant to save the country by raising his baton to strike him, Themistocles merely said 'Strike then, but listen', and Greece triumphed over the Asian tyrant. Scipio[8] was worth as much as any Roman general: Scipio, after conquering Hannibal and Carthage, gloried in serving under the orders of his enemy. O virtue of great hearts! In your presence, what are all the agitations of pride and all the pretensions of small souls? O virtue, are you less necessary for founding a Republic than for governing it in peace? O homeland, have you fewer claims on the representatives of the French people, than Greece and Rome had on their generals? What am I saying? If among us the functions of revolutionary administration are no longer laborious duties but objects of ambition, then the Republic is already lost.

The authority of the National Convention needs to be respected by all Europe; it is to degrade it, it is to wipe it out that the tyrants are exhausting all the resources of their policy, and lavishing their treasure. The Convention needs to take a firm resolution to prefer its own government to that of the London cabinet and all the courts in Europe; for if it does not govern, the tyrants will reign.

And what advantages would they not have in this war of ruse and corruption they are waging on the Republic! All the vices are fighting for them: the Republic only has virtues on its side. Virtues are simple, modest, poor, often ignorant, sometimes rough; they are the prerogative of the unfortunate, and the heritage of the people. Vices are surrounded by every treasure, armed with all the charms of luxury and all the lures of perfidy; they are flanked by all the dangerous talents used for crime.

With what depth of artistry the tyrants turn against us, I will not say our passions and weaknesses, but our very patriotism!

And with what rapidity the seeds of division they throw among us could develop, if we do not hasten to stifle them!

Thanks to five years of betrayal and tyranny, thanks to an excess of improvidence and credulity, thanks to a few robust strokes too readily withdrawn in pusillanimous repentance, Austria, England, Russia, Prussia and Italy have had time to establish a secret government in France, the French government's rival. They too have their committees, their treasury, their agents; that government is acquiring the strength we are removing from our own; it has the unity we have long lacked, the policy we are too inclined to think we can do without, the spirit of consistency, and the concerted approach we have not always felt to be necessary.

And for some time, the foreign courts have been vomiting over France all the cunning scoundrels they have in their pay. Their agents still infest our armies; the very victory at Toulon proves it: it took all the dash of the soldiers, all the fidelity of the generals, all the heroism of the people's representatives, to triumph over that betrayal. They deliberate in our administrations, our section assemblies;[9] they infiltrate our clubs;[10] they have even sat in the sanctuary of national representation; they are controlling and will indefinitely control counter-revolution on the same level.

They prowl about us; they overhear our secrets; they flatter our passions; they seek to influence us even in our opinions; they turn our resolutions against us. Are you weak? They praise your prudence. Are you prudent? They accuse you of weakness; they call your courage temerity; your justice, cruelty. Treat them well, they conspire publicly; threaten them, and they conspire in the shadows, behind a mask of patriotism. Yesterday they were murdering the defenders of liberty; today they are attending their funerals, and demanding divine honours for them, while awaiting the chance to slaughter their fellows. Is it time to ignite civil war? They preach all the follies of superstition. Is the civil war about to be extinguished by the floods of French blood? They abjure their priesthood and their gods to reignite it.

Englishmen, Prussians, have been seen spreading through our towns and countryside, announcing senseless doctrines in the name of the National Convention; unfrocked priests have been seen at the head of seditious gatherings, for which religion was the motive or pretext. Already, patriots led into imprudent acts by hatred of fanaticism alone have been murdered; blood has already flowed in a number of districts as a result of these deplorable quarrels, as if we had too much blood to fight the tyrants of Europe. O shame! O the weakness of human reason! A great nation looking like the plaything of the most despicable lackeys of tyranny!

For some time foreigners have appeared the arbiters of public tranquillity. Money flowed or vanished at their will; when they wished it, the people found bread; mobs formed and dissipated outside bakers' doors at their signal. They surround us with their hired murderers and spies; we know it, we see it, and yet they live! They seem inaccessible to the blade of the law. It is more difficult, even today, to punish an important conspirator than to snatch a friend of liberty from the hands of calumny.

Hardly had we begun to denounce the falsely philosophic excesses provoked by enemies of France; hardly had patriotism pronounced in this chamber the word ultra-revolutionary, to designate them; before the traitors in Lyons,[11] all the partisans of tyranny, hastened to apply it to hot-blooded and generous patriots who had avenged the people and the law. On one hand they are reviving the former system of persecution against friends of the Republic; on the other they plead indulgence for scoundrels dripping with the homeland's blood.

Meanwhile their crimes accumulate; impious cohorts of foreign emissaries are recruited day after day; France is flooded with them; they await, and will await indefinitely, a moment favourable to their sinister designs. They are digging in, billeting themselves in our midst; they are raising new counter-revolutionary redoubts and batteries, while the tyrants who pay them are assembling new armies.

Yes, these perfidious emissaries who talk to us, who flatter us, are the brothers, the accomplices of the ferocious parasites who ravage our crops, who have taken possession of our cities and our vessels bought by their masters, who have massacred our brothers, pitilessly slaughtered our prisoners, our wives, our children, the representatives of the French people. What am I saying? The monsters who committed those crimes are less atrocious than the wretches who tear secretly at our entrails; yet they still breathe, they still conspire unpunished!

They only await leaders to rally them; they are seeking them from among you. Their main object is to set us at odds with each other. That disastrous struggle would raise the hopes of the aristocracy, revive the plots of federalism; it would avenge the Girondin faction for the law that punished its crimes; it would punish the Mountain for its sublime devotion; for it is the Mountain, or rather the Convention, that they are attacking by dividing it and destroying its work.

As for ourselves, we will make war only on the English, the Prussians, the Austrians and their accomplices. It is by exterminating them that we will reply to these libels. We can hate only the enemies of the homeland.

We should strike terror not into the hearts of patriots or unfortunates, but into the dens of foreign brigands where the spoils are shared and the blood of the French people is drunk.

The Committee has noted that the law was not prompt enough in punishing major culprits. Foreigners, known agents of the allied kings; generals stained with the blood of Frenchmen, former accomplices of Dumouriez,[12] Custine and Lamarlière,[13] have been under arrest for some time and have not been tried.

The conspirators are many; they seem to be multiplying, and examples of that sort are rare. Punishing a hundred obscure and subordinate culprits is less useful to liberty than executing the head of a conspiracy.

The members of the Revolutionary Tribunal,[14] whose patriotism and fairness are generally praiseworthy, have themselves pointed out to the Committee of Public Safety the causes that sometimes hamper its workings without making them more certain, and have asked us for the reform of a law still bearing the marks of the unhappy time when it was made. We propose to authorize the Committee to submit some appropriate changes to you, which would also tend to make the workings of justice even more propitious to innocence, and at the same time inescapable for crime and intrigue. You even charged it with this task already, in an earlier decree.

We propose, as of this moment, that you hasten the trial of the foreigners and generals accused of conspiracy with the tyrants who are making war on us.

It is not enough to frighten the enemies of the homeland; its defenders should be helped. We will therefore ask your legal system to include some arrangements in favour of the soldiers who are fighting and suffering for liberty.

The French army is not only the terror of tyrants; it is the glory of the nation and humanity: when marching to victory, our virtuous warriors cry: Long live the Republic; when they fall to enemy steel, their cry is: Long live the Republic. Their last words are hymns to liberty, their last sighs good wishes for the homeland. If all the chiefs had been worthy of the troops, Europe would have been vanquished long ago. Any act of beneficence towards the army is an act of national gratitude.

The assistance given to defenders of the homeland and their families seems to us to be too modest. We believe that it could be increased by a third without problems. The Republic's immense financial resources make this measure possible; the homeland is clamouring for it.

It also seemed to us that crippled soldiers, and the widows and children of those who have died for the homeland, were finding the formalities required by law, the multiplicity of application forms, and sometimes the coldness or malevolence of certain junior officials, difficult enough to delay the enjoyment of the benefits to which the law entitles them. We thought that the remedy to this problem would be to give them unofficial defenders established by law, to help them with the means to secure their rights.

For all these reasons, we submit to you the following decree:

The National Convention decrees:

Article I – The public prosecutor of the Revolutionary Tribunal will without delay bring to trial Dietrich,[15] Custine the son of the general punished by the law, Biron,[16] des Brulys, Barthélemy,[17] and all the generals and officers accused of complicity with Dumouriez, Custine, Lamarlière and Houchard. He will bring to trial in the same way the foreigners, bankers and other individuals charged with treason and connivance with the kings allied against the French Republic.

II – The Committee of Public Safety will report, in the shortest time possible, on ways of improving the organization of the Revolutionary Tribunal.

III – The assistance and compensation payments granted under earlier decrees to defenders of the homeland wounded while fighting for it, or to the widows and children of those killed, are increased by a third.

IV – A commission will be created and charged with facilitating the means to enjoy the benefits to which they are entitled by law.

V – The members of this commission will be appointed by the National Convention, on nomination by the Committee of Public Safety.

14

ON THE PRINCIPLES OF POLITICAL MORALITY THAT SHOULD GUIDE THE NATIONAL CONVENTION IN THE DOMESTIC ADMINISTRATION OF THE REPUBLIC

5 February 1794/18 Pluviôse Year II[1]

In the name of the Committee of Public Safety, Robespierre presented to the Convention the constitutive moral principles for the French government, a month before Saint-Just's Ventôse decrees.[2] The speech was set against the 'contrary factions' on both sides, the 'moderates' (Camille Desmoulins) and the 'ultra-revolutionaries' (Hébert).

Citizen people's representatives,

Some time ago, we laid down the principles of our external policy: we are here today to develop the principles of our internal policy.

After walking aimlessly for some time, and being as it were carried hither and thither by the movement of opposing factions, the representatives of the French people have at last displayed a character and a government. An abrupt change in the nation's fortunes announced to Europe the regeneration that had taken place within the national representation. But it should be acknowledged that up to this very moment we have been guided, in such stormy circumstances, by a love of good and a feeling for the needs of the homeland, rather than by an exact theory and precise rules of conduct, which we had not even the leisure to draw up.

It is time to state clearly the goal of the revolution, and the conclusion we want to reach; it is time for us to list for ourselves both the obstacles that still separate us from it, and the means we should adopt to attain it: a simple and important idea that seems never to have been thought of. Well, how would a cowardly and corrupt government ever have dared to do it? A king, a vainglorious Senate, a Caesar, a Cromwell must above all veil their plans in a religious shroud, compromise with all the vices, flatter all the parties, crush that of the upright men and oppress or deceive the people, to reach the goal of their perfidious ambition. If we had not had a greater task to fulfil, if all that was at issue here were the interests of a faction or a new aristocracy, we might have been able to believe, like certain writers who are more ignorant than perverse, that the plan for the French Revolution was clearly written in the works of Tacitus[3] and Machiavelli,[4] and looked for the duties of people's representatives in the history of Augustus, Tiberius or Vespasian,[5] or even that of some French legislators; for, nuances of perfidy or cruelty apart, all tyrants are alike.

We have come here today to confide your political secrets to the universe, so that all friends of the homeland may rally to the voice of reason and the public interest; so that the French nation and its representatives may be respected in all countries of the universe where knowledge of their real principles can penetrate; so that the plotters who are always seeking to replace other plotters may be judged in accordance with sure and easy rules.

These precautions should be taken in good time to place the destinies of liberty in the hands of truth which is eternal, rather than of men who pass on, in such a way that if the government forgets the people's interests, or falls into the hands of corrupt men, in the natural course of things, the light of acknowledged principles would expose its betrayals, and any new faction would die at the very thought of crime.

Happy is the people that can reach that point! For, whatever new insults are being prepared for it, a few expedients do not suggest an order of things in which public reason is the guarantor of liberty!

What is the goal we are aiming for? Peaceful enjoyment of liberty and equality; the reign of that eternal justice whose laws are engraved, not in marble and stone, but in the hearts of all men, even of the slave who forgets them, and the tyrant who denies them.

We want an order of things in which all base and cruel passions would be fettered, and all beneficent and generous passions awakened by the laws; in which ambition would be a desire to merit glory and serve the homeland; in which distinctions are born only of equality itself; in which the citizen would be subject to the magistrate, the magistrate to the people and the people to justice; in which the homeland would ensure the well-being of every individual, and every individual would share with pride the prosperity and glory of the homeland; in which all souls would grow larger through the continual communication of republican sentiments, and the need to deserve the esteem of a great people; in which the arts would be decorations of the liberty that ennobled them, commerce the source of public wealth and not just the monstrous opulence of a few houses.

We want in our country to substitute morality for egoism, probity for honour, principles for practices, duties for proprieties, the rule of reason for the tyranny of fashion, contempt of vice for contempt of misfortune, pride for insolence, greatness of soul for vanity, love of glory for love of money, good people for good company, merit for intrigue, genius for fine wit, truth for brilliance, the charm of happiness for the boredom of luxury, the greatness of man for the pettiness of great men, a magnanimous, powerful, happy people for an amiable, frivolous and miserable people; in short all the virtues and miracles of the Republic for all the vices and absurdities of monarchy.

We want, in a word, to fulfil nature's wishes, to further the destinies of humanity, to keep the promises of philosophy, to absolve providence of the long reign of crime and tyranny. So that France, once illustrious among enslaved countries, eclipsing the glory of all the free peoples that have existed, may become the model for all nations, the terror of oppressors, the consolation of the oppressed, the ornament of the universe; and that in sealing our work with our blood, we may at least glimpse the shining dawn of universal felicity. That is our ambition, that is our goal.

What nature of government can achieve these prodigies? Only democratic or republican government: these two words are synonymous, despite the abuses of vulgar language; for aristocracy is no more republican than monarchy. A democracy is not a state in which the people, continually assembled, manages all public business for itself, still less one in which a hundred thousand fractions of the people, through isolated, precipitate and contradictory measures, would decide the fate of the whole society: no such government has ever existed, and it could only exist to take the people back to despotism.

Democracy is a state in which the sovereign people, guided by laws which are its own work, does for itself all that it can do properly, and through delegates all that it cannot do for itself.

It is therefore in the principles of democratic government that you should seek rules for your political conduct.

But to found and consolidate democracy among us, to achieve the peaceful rule of constitutional law, we must first end the war of liberty on tyranny and successfully weather the storms of the revolution: such is the goal of the revolutionary system you have adopted. So you should still be adjusting your conduct to the stormy circumstances that surround the republic; and the plan of your administration should be the product of the spirit of revolutionary government, combined with the general principles of democracy.

Now, what is the fundamental principle of democratic or popular government, the essential mainspring that supports it and makes it move? It is virtue; I am talking about the public virtue that worked such prodigies in Greece and Rome, and that should produce far more astonishing ones in republican France; that virtue that is none other than love of the homeland and its laws.

But as the essence of the republic or of democracy is equality, it follows that love of the homeland necessarily embraces love of equality.

It is also true that this sublime sentiment assumes the primacy of the public interest over all individual interests; which implies that love for the homeland also assumes or produces all the virtues: for what are they, but the strength of soul needed to make people capable of such sacrifices? And how could a slave of avarice or ambition, for example, sacrifice his idol to the homeland?

Not only is virtue the soul of democracy; it can only exist in that form of government. Under monarchy, I know of only one individual who can love the homeland, and who does not even need virtue to do it: he is the monarch. The reason for this is that of all the inhabitants of his states, the monarch is the only one to have a homeland. Is he not the sovereign, de facto at least? Is he not in the people's place? And what is the homeland, if not the country where one is a citizen and a member of the sovereign power?

Following the same principle, in aristocratic states the word homeland means something only to the patrician families who have invaded sovereignty.

Only in a democracy is the state truly the homeland of all the individuals in it, and can count as many defenders interested in its cause as there are citizens. That is the reason for the superiority of free peoples over others. Athens and Sparta triumphed over the tyrants of Asia, and the Swiss over the tyrants of Spain and Austria; there is no need to look for any other reason why.

But the French are the first people in the world to have established true democracy, by calling all men to equality and the plenitude of citizens' rights; and that, in my opinion, is the reason why all the tyrants allied against the Republic will be vanquished.

At this point there are some important conclusions to draw from the principles we have laid out.

Since the soul of the Republic is virtue, equality, and your goal is to found and consolidate the Republic, it follows that the first rule of your political conduct should be to relate all your operations to the maintenance of equality and the development of virtue; for the legislator's first care should be to strengthen the principle of government. Thus, anything that tends to arouse love of the homeland, to purify morals, to elevate souls, to direct the passions of the human heart towards the public interest, should be adopted or established by you. Anything that tends to concentrate them on the abjectness of the personal self, to arouse crazes for small things and contempt for great ones, should be rejected or repressed by you. In the French Revolution's system, that which is immoral is impolitic, that which is corrupting is counter-revolutionary. Weakness, vices, prejudices are the path of royalty. Led too often perhaps by the weight of our old habits, as well as the imperceptible slope of human weakness, towards false ideas and pusillanimous sentiments, we need to defend ourselves far less against excesses of energy than excesses of weakness. Perhaps the most dangerous reef we have to avoid is not the fervour of excessive zeal, but rather the lassitude of well-being, and fear of our own courage. So ceaselessly refit the sacred mainspring of republican government, instead of letting it drop. There is no need to add that I do not mean here to justify any excesses. Even the most sacred principles can be abused; it is for the wisdom of the government to examine circumstances, seize moments, choose ways and means; for the manner in which great things are prepared is an essential part of the talent for achieving them, as wisdom is itself a part of virtue.

We do not aspire to force the French Republic into the mould of the Spartan one; we do not want to give it either the austerity, or the corruption, of the cloisters. We have laid out for you, in all its purity, the moral and political principle of people's government. So you have a compass that can guide you amid the storms of all the passions and the whirlwind of intrigues that surround you. You have a touchstone against which you can assess all your laws, all the propositions that are put to you. By comparing them continuously with that principle, you can henceforth avoid the ordinary pitfalls of large assemblies, the danger of unexpected attacks and of hurried, incoherent and contradictory measures. You can give all your operations the cohesion, unity, wisdom and dignity that should characterize the representatives of the world's foremost people.

The easy consequences of the principle of democracy have no need to be spelt out; what deserves to be developed is the simple and fertile principle itself.

Republican virtue can be considered in relation to the people, and in relation to the government: it is necessary in both cases. When the government alone is deprived of it, there remains a reservoir in the people; but when the people itself is corrupt, liberty is already lost.

Happily, virtue is natural to the people, whatever aristocratic prejudice may think. A nation is really corrupted when, having lost by slow degrees its character and its liberty, it moves from democracy to aristocracy or monarchy; that is the death of the body politic through decrepitude. When after four hundred years of glory avarice finally chased morality out of Sparta with Lycurgus's laws,[6] Agis[7] died in vain to have them repealed! Demosthenes could thunder all he liked against Philip,[8] Philip could find lawyers in the stews of degenerate Athens who were more eloquent than Demosthenes. Athens still has as many inhabitants as in the time of Miltiades[9] and Aristides;[10] but there are no Athenians among them. What matter that Brutus has slain the tyrant? Tyranny lives on in human hearts, and Rome exists only in Brutus.

But when, through prodigious efforts of courage and reason, a people breaks the fetters of despotism to make them the trophies of liberty; when, through the strength of its moral temperament, it returns, so to speak, from death's embrace to resume all the vigour of youth; when, by turns sensitive and proud, intrepid and docile, it can be stopped neither by the indestructible ramparts nor the numberless armies of the tyrants armed against it, and stops of its own accord before the image of the law;

then if such a people does not soar rapidly to the height of its destiny, it can only be through the fault of those who govern it.

Besides, one might say that in a sense, the people has no need of great virtue to love justice and equality; it is enough that it love itself.

But the magistrate is obliged to sacrifice his own interest to the people's interest, and the pride of power to equality. The law needs to speak with authority above all to those who are its instruments. The government needs to press down on itself, to keep all its parts in harmony with equality. If there is a representative body, a primary authority constituted by the people, it has the continuous task of supervising and repressing all public officials. But who will repress the body itself, if not its own virtue? The more elevated that source of public order is, the purer it should be; so the representative body needs to start with itself, by subjecting all its private passions to the general passion for public good. Happy are the representatives when their glory and their very interests, as well as their duty, attach them to the cause of liberty!

From all of this we should deduce a great truth: that the character of popular government is to be trusting towards the people and severe with itself.

Here the whole development of our theory would end, if you only had to steer the vessel of the Republic in calm waters; but the tempest howls; and the stage of revolution in which you are at present imposes another task.

That great purity of the foundations of the French Revolution, the very sublimity of its objective, is exactly what gives us our strength, but also our weakness: our strength, because it gives us the ascendancy of truth over fraud, and of the rights of the public interest over private interests; our weakness, because it rallies against us all vicious men, all those who in their hearts meditate plundering the people, and those who want to escape unpunished after plundering it, and those who reject liberty as a personal calamity, and those who embrace the revolution as a trade and the Republic as prey: hence the defection of so many ambitious or greedy men who, since our beginning, have deserted us on the road, for they had not started the journey with the same destination in mind. One might say that the two opposed spirits that have been represented as disputing the dominion of nature are fighting during this great epoch of human history to decide the destinies of the world once and for all, and that France is the theatre of that formidable struggle. Outside, all the tyrants surround you; within, all the friends of tyranny are conspiring; they will conspire until hope has been stripped from crime. We must stifle the internal and external enemies of the Republic, or perish with it; and in this situation, the first maxim of your policy should be that the people are led by reason, and the enemies of the people by terror.

If the mainspring of popular government in peacetime is virtue, the mainspring of popular government in revolution is virtue and terror both: virtue, without which terror is disastrous; terror, without which virtue is powerless. Terror is nothing but prompt, severe, inflexible justice; it is therefore an emanation of virtue; it is not so much a specific principle as a consequence of the general principle of democracy applied to the homeland's most pressing needs.

It has been said that terror was the mainspring of despotic government. So does yours resemble despotism? Yes, as the sword shining in the hands of the heroes of liberty resembles the one wielded by tyranny's satellites. Let the despot govern his stupefied subjects through terror; he is right, as a despot: intimidate by terror the enemies of liberty; and you will be right, as founders of the Republic. The revolution's government is the despotism of liberty over tyranny. Is strength made only for the protection of crime? And are not thunderbolts meant to strike vainglorious heads?

Nature's law is that any physical and moral entity must provide for its own preservation; crime murders innocence to reign, and innocence in the hands of crime struggles with all its might.

Let tyranny reign for a single day; the next day not a patriot will remain. For how long will the rage of despots be called justice, and the people's justice be called barbarity or rebellion? How tender people are towards oppressors and how inexorable towards the oppressed! Nothing could be more natural: who does not hate crime cannot love virtue.

One or the other must succumb, however. Indulgence for the royalists, cry certain people. Mercy for scoundrels! No: mercy for the innocent, mercy for the weak, mercy for the unfortunate, mercy for humanity!

Social protection is due only to peaceful citizens; there are no citizens but republicans in the Republic. Royalists and conspirators are foreign to it, or rather they are enemies. Is not the terrible war waged by liberty on tyranny indivisible? Are not the enemies within allies of the enemies without? Assassins who ravage the homeland from the inside; intriguers who buy the consciences of people's representatives, and the traitors who sell them; mercenary scribblers bribed to dishonour the people's cause, to kill public virtue, to stoke the flames of civil dissension, to clear the way for political counter-revolution with moral counter-revolution; are all these people less culpable or less dangerous than the tyrants they serve? All who interpose their parricidal gentleness between these scoundrels and the avenging sword of national justice resemble those who would rush between the tyrants' henchmen and our soldiers' bayonets; all the fervours of their fake sensibility seem to me nothing but languishing sighs, directed towards England or Austria.

Well! For whom then could they be feeling such tenderness? Could it be for two hundred thousand heroes, the nation's élite, mown down by the steel of enemies of liberty or the daggers of royal or federalist assassins? No, those were only plebeians, patriots; to have a right to their tender interest you would have to be at least the widow of a general who has betrayed the homeland twenty times; to obtain their indulgence, you almost have to prove that you have sacrificed ten thousand Frenchmen, as a Roman general, I believe, had to have killed ten thousand enemies to obtain a triumph. They listen unmoved to the catalogue of horrors committed by tyrants against the defenders of liberty; our women horribly mutilated; our children massacred at their mothers' breasts; our prisoners expiating their touching and sublime heroism with horrible torments: yet they call it horrid butchery, the long-delayed punishment of a few monsters grown fat on the homeland's purest blood.

They bear patiently the misery of citizenesses who have sacrificed their brothers, their children, their husbands to the finest of all causes; but they lavish the most generous consolations on the wives of conspirators; it is accepted that they can charm justice unpunished, and contrary to liberty plead the causes of their husbands and their accomplices; they have been made almost into a privileged guild, creditor and pensioner of the people.

How good-natured we are, to be still duped by words! As aristocracy and moderantism still govern us through the murderous maxims they have given us!

The aristocracy is better defended by its intrigues than patriotism by its services. We want to govern revolutions with palace quibbles; we deal with conspiracies against the Republic like trials of individuals. Tyranny kills, and liberty pleads; and the code made by the conspirators themselves is the law by which they are judged.

Even with the salvation of the homeland at stake, the testimony of the universe cannot stand in for witness evidence, nor the obvious facts for documentary evidence.

The slowness of the trials is equivalent to impunity; uncertainty over sentences encourages all the culprits; and still people complain about the severity of justice; they complain about the detention of enemies of the Republic. They seek their examples in the history of tyrants, because they do not want to choose them from that of peoples, or draw them from the spirit of threatened liberty. In Rome, when the consul discovered the conspiracy and snuffed it out immediately with the death of Catalina's[11] accomplices, by whom was he accused of having violated the proper forms? By the ambitious Caesar, who wished to swell his party with the horde of plotters, Piso, Clodius,[12] all the bad citizens who feared for themselves the virtue of a true Roman and the severity of the law.

To punish the oppressors of humanity: that is clemency; to forgive them, that is barbarity. The rigour of tyrants has rigour as its sole principle: that of republican government is based on beneficence.

So, bad cess to him who would dare turn on the people the terror that should fall only on its enemies! Bad cess to him who, confusing the inevitable mistakes of public-spiritedness with the calculated errors of perfidy, or with the attacks of conspirators, abandons the dangerous plotter to prosecute the peaceful citizen! Perish the villain who dares to abuse the sacred name of liberty, or the formidable weapons it has entrusted to him, to strike bereavement and death into the hearts of patriots! This abuse has taken place, it cannot be denied. It has been exaggerated, no doubt, by the aristocracy: but even if there existed in the whole Republic just one virtuous man persecuted by enemies of the Republic, the government's duty would be to search anxiously for him, and avenge him in proper style.

But are we to conclude from these persecutions directed at patriots by the hypocritical zeal of counter-revolutionaries, that counter-revolutionaries should be set at liberty and severity renounced? These new crimes by the aristocracy simply demonstrate the need for severity. What does the boldness of our enemies show, if not the weakness with which they have been prosecuted? This is due in large part to the relaxed doctrine that has been preached recently to reassure them. If you were to listen to that advice, your enemies would reach their goal and receive from your own hands the price of the last of their crimes.

How frivolous it would be to regard a few victories won by patriotism as the end of all our dangers! Take a glance at our true situation: you will feel that vigilance and energy are more necessary to you than ever. A veiled malevolence counters the government's operations everywhere:

the deadly influence of foreign courts may be more hidden, but is just as active, just as disastrous. You can feel that crime intimidated has merely covered its workings with greater skill.

The internal enemies of the French people have split into two factions, as if into two army corps. They march under banners of different colours and by different routes: but they march towards the same goal; that goal is the disorganization of the popular government, the ruin of the Convention, in other words the triumph of tyranny. One of those two factions pushes us towards weakness, the other towards excess. One wants to change liberty into a bacchante, the other into a prostitute.

Minor plotters, quite often good citizens who have been deceived, side with one or the other party: but the leaders belong to the cause of the kings or aristocracy and always unite against the patriots. Rogues, even when making war on each other, hate each other far less than they detest decent people. The homeland is their quarry; they fight each other for shares of it; but they are in league against those who defend it.

One party has been given the name of moderates; perhaps there is more wit than accuracy in the term ultra-revolutionaries which is used to designate the other. This name, which cannot be applied in any case to men of good faith whose zeal and ignorance may have carried them beyond sound revolutionary policy, is not an exact description of the perfidious men whom tyranny has bribed to compromise the sacred principles of our revolution, by applying them in a false and disastrous manner.

The fake revolutionary is perhaps more often behind the revolution than ahead of it: he is moderate; he is crazy about patriotism, depending on circumstances. What he is going to think the next day is decided in Prussian, English, Austrian and even Muscovite committees. He opposes energetic measures and exaggerates the ones he has failed to prevent; severe towards innocence, but indulgent towards crime; even accusing culprits if they are too poor to buy his silence and too unimportant to deserve his zeal; but careful never to compromise himself to the point of defending slandered virtue; sometimes uncovering uncovered plots, tearing the masks off unmasked or even decapitated traitors, but strongly recommending traitors who are still alive and of good standing; always eager to flatter prevailing opinion, and no less careful never to throw light on it, and above all never to offend it; always ready to adopt bold measures, provided they have a lot of drawbacks; slandering those that offer nothing but advantages, or cluttering them with amendments to render them harmful; speaking the truth with economy, only as much as necessary to acquire the right to lie with impunity; distilling the good a drop at a time, and pouring out the bad in torrents; full of fire for grand resolutions that mean nothing; more than indifferent to those that may honour the people's cause and save the homeland; much given to the forms of patriotism; very attached, like the devout whose enemy he declares himself, to foreign ways, he would rather wear out a hundred red caps than perform one good act.

What difference do you find between those people and your moderates? They are servants employed by the same master or, if you like, accomplices who pretend to be at odds the better to hide their crimes. Judge them, not by the difference of language, but by the sameness of the results. The one who attacks the National Convention in rabid speeches and the one who deceives it to compromise it, are they not in agreement? The same one who with unjust rigours forces patriotism to tremble for its safety, invokes amnesty for the aristocracy and treason. Another called on France to conquer the world, with no other aim than calling on the tyrants to conquer France. The hypocritical foreigner who for five years past has proclaimed Paris the capital of the globe[13] was just expressing in different jargon the anathemas of the vile federalists wishing destruction on Paris. Preaching atheism is merely a way of absolving superstition and accusing philosophy; and declaring war on divinity is only a diversion in favour of royalty.

What other method remains for fighting liberty? Will anyone follow the example of the first champions of aristocracy by praising the sweetness of servitude and the benefits of monarchy, the supernatural genius and incomparable virtues of kings?

Are they going to proclaim the vanity of the rights of man and of the principles of eternal justice?

Are they going to exhume the nobility and the clergy, or assert the imprescriptible right of the upper bourgeoisie to succeed them both?

No. It is much easier to don the mask of patriotism and disfigure the sublime drama of the revolution with insolent parodies, to compromise the cause of liberty with hypocritical moderation or studied nonsense.

So the aristocracy is establishing itself in popular societies; counter-revolutionary pride conceals its plots and daggers under ragged clothes; fanaticism smashes its own altars; royalism exults in the Republic's victories; the nobility, weighed down with memories, tenderly embraces equality in order to stifle it; tyranny, stained with the blood of liberty's defenders, heaps flowers on their tombs. If not all hearts have changed, how many faces are masked! How many traitors meddle in our affairs only to wreck them!

Do you want to put them to the test? Instead of oaths and declamations, ask them for real services.

Do we need to act? They perorate. Do we need to deliberate? They want to act first. Are the times peaceful? They will oppose any useful change. Are they stormy? They will talk of reforming everything, to overturn everything. Do you want to contain the rebels? They remind you of Caesar's clemency. Do you want to save patriots from persecution? They suggest Brutus's firmness as a model. They discover that someone used to be a noble when he is serving the Republic; they remember it no longer when he betrays it. Is peace useful? They draw your attention to the palms of victory. Is war necessary? They praise the sweetness of peace. Does the territory need to be defended? They want to cross the mountains and the seas to chastise tyrants. Do our fortresses need to be retaken? They want to take churches by storm and escalade heaven. They forget the Austrians to make war on the devout. Does our cause need the loyal support of our allies? They will declaim against all the governments in the world and suggest that you bring to trial the Great Mughal himself. Is the people going to the Capitol to thank the gods for its victories? They intone lugubrious dirges on our past reverses. Are new victories on the cards? They spread among us hatreds, divisions, persecution and discouragement. Should we achieve people's sovereignty and concentrate its strength in a strong and respected government? They find that the principles of government are damaging to the people's sovereignty. Do we need to assert the rights of the people oppressed by the government? They speak only of respect for the law and obedience to the constituted authorities.

They have found an admirable expedient for seconding the efforts of the republican government: disrupt it, degrade it completely, make war on the patriots who have contributed to our success.

Are you seeking means to provision your armies? Are you trying to snatch from avarice and fear the supplies they are keeping scarce? They moan patriotically about public misery and announce a famine. The wish to forestall evil is always to them a reason for augmenting it. In the North the poultry were killed, depriving us of eggs, under the pretext that poultry eat grain. In the Midi, people wanted to uproot mulberry and orange trees, on the pretext that silk is a luxury product, and oranges unnecessary.

You could never imagine some of the excesses committed by hypocritical counter-revolutionaries to blacken the cause of the revolution. Would you believe that in the areas where superstition has had most influence, not content with loading the operations concerning religion with all the forms most calculated to render them odious, they spread terror among the people by starting a rumour that all children under ten and all old people over seventy were going to be killed? That this rumour was spread particularly in former Brittany and in the departments of Rhine and Moselle? This is one of the crimes imputed to the former public prosecutor of the Strasbourg criminal tribunal. The tyrannical follies of this man make the stories about Caligula and Heliogabalus seem convincing;[14] but they are hard to believe, even after seeing the evidence. He carried his frenzy to the point of requisitioning women for his own use; they say he even employed this method to get married. Where did it come from all of a sudden, that swarm of foreigners, priests, nobles and intriguers of every sort, which at the same moment spread across the surface of the Republic to carry out, in the name of philosophy, a plan of counter-revolution that could only be stopped by the strength of public reason? An execrable design, worthy of the genius of the foreign courts allied against liberty and the depravity of the Republic's internal enemies!

That is how, to the continual miracles wrought by the virtue of a great people, intrigue always adds the baseness of its criminal schemes, a baseness ordered by tyrants, later using it as material for their ridiculous manifestos, to hold ignorant peoples in the filth of opprobrium and the chains of servitude.

But, ha! What can the crimes of its enemies really do to liberty? When the sun is veiled by a passing cloud, does it stop being the star that animates nature? Does the impure scum that the Ocean leaves on its shores make it any less imposing?

In perfidious hands all the remedies for our ills become poisons; whatever you can do, whatever you can say, they will turn it against you, even the truths we have just been developing.

Thus, for example, after having planted the seeds of civil war everywhere, with the violent attack on religious prejudices, they will seek to arm fanaticism and aristocracy with the very measures that sound policy recommended to you in favour of freedom of religion. If you had given the conspiracy a free rein, sooner or later it would have produced a terrible and universal reaction; if you stop it, they will still try to profit from it, by arguing that you are protecting priests and moderates. It should not even astonish you if the authors of that scheme turn out to be the priests who have confessed their charlatanism most boldly.

If patriots, carried away by a pure but unthinking zeal, have been taken in here or there by their intrigues, they will put all the blame on those patriots; for the main point of their Machiavellian doctrine is to do away with the Republic, by doing away with the republicans, as one subjugates a country by destroying the army that defends it. From this one can understand one of their favoured principles, which is that men should be considered of no account; a maxim of royal origin, which means that all the friends of liberty should be left to them.

It is apparent that the destiny of men who seek only the public good is to become the victims of those who are self-seeking, something that has two causes: firstly, that intriguers attack with the vices of the old régime; secondly, that patriots only defend themselves with the virtues of the new one.

Such an internal situation should appear worthy of all your attention, especially when you reflect that at the same time you have the tyrants of Europe to fight, twelve hundred thousand men under arms to maintain, and that the government is obliged continually to repair, by force of energy and vigilance, all the ills that the numberless multitude of our enemies has prepared for us in the course of five years.

What is the remedy for all these ills? We know of none but the development of that general mainspring of the Republic: virtue.

Democracy perishes through two excesses, the aristocracy of those who govern, or the people's contempt for the authorities it has itself established, a contempt that results in each coterie, each individual appropriating public power, and brings the people, through excess of disorder, to annihilation or rule by a single individual.

The double task of the moderates and the fake revolutionaries is to pull us perpetually back and forth between these two reefs.

But the people's representatives can avoid them both; for the government is always capable of being just and wise; and when it has that character, it is sure of the people's confidence.

It is certainly true that the goal of all our enemies is to dissolve the Convention; it is true that the tyrant of Great Britain and his allies have promised their parliament and subjects to rob you of your energy and the public confidence it has earned you; and that that is the primary instruction given to all their stewards.

But it is a truth that should be regarded as trivial in politics, that a great body invested with the confidence of a great people can only be ruined by its own hand; your enemies are not unaware of it, so you cannot doubt that they are applying themselves primarily to arousing among you all the passions that may forward their sinister plans.

What can they do against the national representation, if they do not manage to catch it in impolitic acts that might supply pretexts for their criminal ranting? They must therefore inevitably want to have two types of agent, one that will seek to degrade the representation in their speeches, the other, in its very heart, that will strive to mislead it, to compromise its glory and the Republic's interests.

To attack it successfully, it was useful to start the civil war against the representatives in the departments that had justified your confidence, and against the Committee of Public Safety; so they were attacked by men who appeared to be fighting between themselves.

How could they do better than to paralyse the Convention government and jam all its machinery, at the moment that should decide the fate of the Republic and the tyrants?

Far be it from us to entertain the idea that there might still exist among us a single man cowardly enough to want to serve the tyrants' cause! Still less would we consider the crime, for which we would never be forgiven, of deceiving the National Convention, and betraying the French people through culpable silence! For it is a happy thing for a free people that the truth, which is the scourge of despots, is always its strength and its salvation. It is true that there still exists a threat to our liberty, perhaps the only serious threat it still has to face: that danger is a plan that existed to rally all the Republic's enemies by reviving the spirit of party; to persecute patriots, to discourage, to ruin loyal agents of republican government, to ensure the failure of the more essential parts of the public service. They tried to deceive the Convention about men and things; they tried to mislead it on the causes of the abuses they exaggerate to render them irremediable; they took great pains to fill its ears with groundless terrors, to send it off course and paralyse it; they seek to divide it; they sought especially to divide the representatives on mission to the departments and the Committee of Public Safety; they tried to induce the first group to rescind measures decreed by the central authority, to cause disorder and confusion; they tried to embitter them on their return, to make them the unknowing instruments of a faction. The foreigners turn all individual passions to their advantage, even deceived patriotism. At first they favoured heading straight for their goal, by slandering the Committee of Public Safety; at the time they were boasting openly that it would collapse under the weight of its arduous functions. The victory and good luck of the French people defended it. Since that time, they have chosen to flatter it while paralysing it and destroying the fruit of its labours. All that vague ranting against the Committee's necessary agents; all the plans for disorganization, disguised under the name of reforms, and already rejected by the Convention, today being reproduced with a strange affectation; that eagerness to recommend intriguers whom the Committee of Public Safety has had to remove; that terror aroused in good citizens; that indulgence with which conspirators are caressed, that whole system of fraud and intrigue, whose principal author is a man you have expelled from your midst,[15] is directed against the National Convention, and tends to fulfil the wishes of all enemies of France.

Since the time when that system was announced in the scurrilous sheets, and implemented through public acts, aristocracy and royalism have started to raise an insolent head, patriotism has been persecuted anew in part of the Republic, and national authority has met with a resistance for which the intriguers were starting to lose the knack. Besides, even if these indirect attacks had no other drawback than dividing the attention and energy of those who have to bear the immense burden you have placed on them, so that they are too often distracted from great public safety measures by the need to expose dangerous intrigues, they could still be considered a diversion useful to our enemies.

But let us take heart; this is the sanctuary of truth; here reside the founders of the Republic, the avengers of humanity and destroyers of tyrants.

Here, to destroy an abuse, it suffices to point it out. For advice on the pride or weakness of individuals, all we have to do is call, in the name of the homeland, on the virtue and glory of the National Convention.

On all the objects of its anxieties and all that might influence the progress of the revolution, we instigate solemn discussion; we entreat it not to allow any individual and hidden interest to usurp here the ascendancy of the Assembly's general will and the indestructible power of reason.

We will limit ourselves today to proposing that you endorse with your formal approval the moral and political truths on which your domestic administration and the stability of the Republic should be based, as you have already endorsed the principles of your conduct towards foreign peoples: in that way you will rally all good citizens, you will deprive the conspirators of hope; you will ensure your advance, and you will confound the intrigues and calumnies of kings; you will honour your cause and your character in the eyes of all peoples.

Give the French people this new pledge of your zeal in protecting patriotism, your inflexible justice for culprits and your devotion to the people's cause. Order that the principles of political morality we have developed here be proclaimed, in your name, inside and outside the Republic.

15

EXTRACTS FROM SPEECH OF 8 THERMIDOR YEAR II

26 July 1794/8 Thermidor Year II[1]

With this speech, Robespierre reappeared at the tribune of the Convention after a long absence. He appeals here to the Assembly, most of whose members he still believes to be 'pure', against the conspiracy that is being spun against him. These were to prove to be Robespierre's last words in public before his arrest on 9 Thermidor.

Citizens,

Let others draw you flattering pictures; I am here to speak useful truths. I am not here to implement any ridiculous terrors put about by perfidy; but I want, if possible, to snuff out the torches of discord with the force of truth alone. *I am going to reveal abuses that tend to the ruin of the homeland and that only your probity can repress.* I am going to defend before you your own flouted authority, and violated liberty. *If I also say something on the persecutions of which I am the object, you will not see it as a crime; you have nothing in common with the tyrants you are fighting.* The cries of outraged innocence do not trouble your ears, and you are well aware that this cause is not one that leaves you unaffected.

The revolutions that, until ours, changed the faces of empires had as their objective only a change of dynasty, or the passage from rule by a single individual to rule by several. The French Revolution is the first to have been based on the theory of the rights of humanity and the principles of justice. Other revolutions only required ambition; ours imposes virtues. Ignorance and force absorbed them into new despotisms; ours, which came from justice, can rest only in its bosom. The Republic, brought gradually into being by the force of things and by the struggle waged by friends of liberty against constantly renewed conspiracies, slipped so to speak through all the factions; but it found their power organized around it, and all the means of influence in their hands; so it has been persecuted constantly since its birth in the persons of the men of good faith who fought for it. The thing was that to keep the advantage of their position, the heads of the factions and their agents were obliged to hide behind the form of the Republic; Précy in Lyons and Brissot in Paris used to cry *Long live the Republic!* All the plotters even adopted the expressions, the rallying words of patriotism, with more eagerness than anyone else. The Austrian, whose job was to fight the revolution; and the Orléanais, whose role was to play the patriot, found themselves in the same battle line, and neither one could be distinguished from the republican. They did not fight our principles, they corrupted them; they never blasphemed against the Revolution, they tried to dishonour it under the pretext of serving it; they declaimed against tyrants, and conspired for tyranny; they praised the Republic, and slandered republicans. The friends of liberty seek to overthrow the power of tyrants with the strength of truth; tyrants seek to destroy the defenders of liberty with calumny; they give the name of tyranny to the very ascendancy of the principles of truth. When that system has managed to prevail, liberty is lost; nothing is legitimate but perfidy and nothing criminal but virtue, for it is in the very nature of things that wherever men assemble there is an influence, either of tyranny or of reason. When reason is proscribed as a crime, tyranny reigns; when good citizens are condemned to silence, then obviously scoundrels must rule. [. . .]

[. . .] No, we were not too severe: I cite in evidence the Republic, which lives! I cite the national representation surrounded with the respect due to the representatives of a great people! I cite the patriots who still groan in the dungeons the scoundrels have opened for them! I cite the new crimes of the enemies of our liberty, and the culpable perseverance of the tyrants in league against us! They talk about our rigour, and the homeland reproaches us for our weakness.

Is it we who threw patriots into dungeons, and carried terror to all conditions of men? It is the monsters who have accused us. Is it we who, ignoring the crimes of the aristocracy and protecting traitors, declared war on peaceable citizens, labelled as crimes either incurable prejudices or things of no account, to find guilty men everywhere, and make the Revolution dreadful to the people itself? It is the monsters who have accused us. Is it we who, seeking out ancient opinions, the fruit of the obsession with traitors, threatened the greater part of the National Convention with the blade, called in the popular societies for the heads of six hundred people's representatives? It is the monsters who have accused us. [. . .]

Such is nevertheless the basis of these schemes for dictatorship and attacks on national liberty, imputed at first to the Committee of Public Safety in general. By what misfortune was this major accusation shifted all of a sudden onto the head of just one of its members? A strange project for one man, to persuade the Convention to cut its throat in detail with its own hands to clear his path to absolute power! Let others see the ridiculous side of these charges; I can see only their atrocity. You will give an *account* at least of your frightful perseverance in pursuing the plan to slaughter all the friends of the homeland, you monsters who seek to rob me of the esteem of the National Convention, the most glorious prize for the work of a mortal being, and one I neither usurped nor snatched, but had been forced to win over! To appear an object of terror in the eyes of what he reveres and loves is, for a man of feeling and probity, the most dreadful of tortures; to make him suffer it is the most heinous of crimes. But I call for your fullest indignation on the atrocious manoeuvres used to shore up these extravagant calumnies. [. . .]

They aspire, it is said, to supreme power; they are exercising it already . . . So the National Convention does not exist! So the French people is annihilated! Stupid slanderers! Have you noticed that your ridiculous rantings are not an insult addressed to an individual, but to an invincible nation which tames and punishes kings? For myself, I would feel extreme repugnance at defending myself personally in front of you against the most cowardly of all tyrannies, if you were not convinced that you are the real objects of these attacks by the enemies of the Republic. Ha! Who am I to be worthy of their persecutions, if they were not part of the general scheme of their conspiracy against the National Convention? Have you not noticed that to isolate you from the nation, they proclaimed to the whole universe that you were dictators ruling by terror, and disowned by the tacit wishes of the French? Did they not call our armies *the Convention hordes* and the French Revolution *Jacobinism*? And when they pretend to give gigantic and ridiculous importance to a weak individual exposed to the insults of all factions, what could their goal be if not to divide you, to degrade you by denying your very existence, in the same way that an impious man denies the existence of the Divinity he fears?

Yet that word *dictatorship* has magical effects; it blackens liberty; it disparages the government, it destroys the Republic; it degrades all the revolutionary institutions, which are presented as the work of a single man; it brings odium on national law, which it presents as being instituted by the ambition of a single man; it concentrates all the hatreds and daggers of fanaticism and aristocracy on that point.

What terrible use the enemies of the Republic have made of the simple name of a Roman magistrature! And if their erudition is so deadly to us, what of their treasure and their plots? I say nothing of their armies; but may I be permitted to send back to the Duke of York and all the royal writers the patents of this ridiculous dignity, which they were the first to send to me. When kings who are not certain of keeping their own crowns assume the right to distribute them to others, they show too much insolence! I understand that a ridiculous prince, or that species of filthy and sacred animal still called kings, might revel in their baseness and take pride in their ignominy; I can understand that George's son, for example, might feel regret for the French sceptre he is strongly suspected of having coveted, and I sympathize sincerely with that modern Tantalus.[2] I will even confess to the shame, not of my homeland, but of the traitors she has punished, that I have seen unworthy representatives of the people who might have exchanged that glorious title for that of manservant to George or d'Orléans. But that a people's representative who feels the dignity of that sacred title, that a French citizen worthy of the name could lower his vows to the culpable and ridiculous grandeurs he has helped to strike down, that he could subject himself to civic degradation to sink to the infamy of the throne, is something that will only seem believable to those twisted beings who have not even the right to believe in virtue! I said, *virtue*! It is a natural passion, no doubt about it; but how would they know it, those venal souls who only ever open themselves to cowardly and ferocious passions; those miserable schemers who never linked patriotism with any moral idea, who marched in the Revolution behind some important and ambitious character, behind I know not what despised prince, like our lackeys in times past in the footsteps of their masters? But there do exist, I can assure you, souls that are feeling and pure; it exists, that tender, imperious and irresistible passion, the torment and delight of magnanimous hearts; that deep horror of tyranny, that compassionate zeal for the oppressed, that sacred love for the homeland, that even more sublime and holy love for humanity, without which a great revolution is just a noisy crime that destroys another crime; it does exist, that generous ambition to establish here on earth the world's first republic. That selfishness of men who are not debased, which finds a celestial delight in the calm of a clear conscience and the ravishing spectacle of public happiness, you can feel it at this moment burning in your souls; I feel it in mine. But how would our vile slanderers ever guess it? How would one born blind have the idea of light? Nature has denied them a soul; they have some right to doubt not just the immortality of the soul, but its very existence.

They call me a tyrant . . . If I were one, they would grovel at my feet, I would stuff them with gold, I would guarantee them the right to commit any and every crime, and they would be grateful. If I were one, the kings we have vanquished, instead of denouncing me (what a tender interest they take in our liberty!) would lend me their culpable support; I would compromise with them. In their distress, what do they want if it is not the help of a faction protected by them, and willing to sell them our country's glory and liberty? Tyranny is achieved through the help of rogues; where are those who fight them going? To the tomb and immortality. What tyrant is protecting me? To what faction do I belong? It is yourselves. What is the faction that since the beginning of the Revolution has put down factions, has got rid of so many accredited traitors? It is you, it is the people; it is principle. That is the faction to which I am pledged, and against which all crimes are in league.

It is you who are being persecuted, it is the homeland, it is all friends of the homeland. I am still defending myself. How many others have been oppressed in the shadows? Who will ever again dare serve the homeland, when I am obliged to reply here to such calumnies? They cite the most natural effects of public spirit and liberty as proof of ambitious scheming; the moral influence of former athletes of the Revolution is now compared by them to tyranny. You are yourselves the most cowardly of all tyrants, you who slander the power of truth! What do you want, you who would like truth to be powerless on the lips of representatives of the French people? Truth undoubtedly has its power, it has its anger, its own despotism; it has touching accents and terrible ones, that resound with force in pure hearts as in guilty consciences, and that untruth can no more imitate than Salome can imitate the thunderbolts of heaven; but accuse nature of it, accuse the people, which wants it and loves it.

There are two powers on earth, reason and tyranny; wherever one is predominant, the other is banned. Those who denounce the moral strength of reason as a crime are therefore seeking to revive tyranny. If you do not want the defenders of principle to obtain some influence in the difficult struggle of liberty against intrigue, then you want victory to go to intrigue. If the people's representatives who defend the people's cause cannot obtain its esteem without being punished, what will be the consequence of that system, except that serving the people will no longer be permitted, the Republic will be proscribed and tyranny restored? And what tyranny is more odious than one that punishes the people in the persons of its defenders? For the thing that is most free in the world, even when despotism reigns, is friendship, is it not? But you, who make it a crime in our case, are you envious of it? No, you prize nothing but the gold and perishable goods that tyrants lavish on those who serve them. You are serving them, if you corrupt public morality and protect every crime; the safeguard of conspirators lies in neglect of principle and in corruption; that of defenders of liberty lies in public awareness. You are serving them if, always on this side or that of the truth, you preach by turns now the aristocracy's treacherous moderation, and now the furious passion of false democrats. You are serving them, if you stubbornly continue to preach atheism and vice. You want to destroy representation if you degrade it through your conduct and disrupt it with your intrigues. Which is the more guilty, one who threatens its security through violence, or one who undermines its justice through seduction and perfidy? To mislead it is to betray it; to push it into acts contrary to its intentions and principles is to risk its destruction; for its power is based on virtue itself and on the confidence of the nation. We cherish it, we who, having fought for its physical security, are today defending its glory and its principles! Is that the way to despotism? What a cruel mockery it is to brand as despots citizens who are still proscribed! And what else are those who have steadfastly defended their country's interests? The Republic has triumphed, but never its defenders. Who am I, who stand here accused? A slave of liberty, a living martyr of the Republic, as much the victim of crime as its enemy. All rogues offend me; what others see as the most unimportant, the most legitimate actions, are crimes to me. A man is slandered just because he knows me. Others are forgiven their offences; my zeal is labelled a crime. Take my consciousness away, I am the most unhappy of men; I do not even enjoy the rights of a citizen. What am I saying? I am not even allowed to perform the duties of a people's representative. [. . .]

A particular effort was made to prove that the Revolutionary Tribunal was a bloodthirsty tribunal, created by me alone, and that I controlled it absolutely to have all the good people slaughtered and even all the scoundrels, because people wanted to give me enemies of all kinds. That cry resounded in all the prisons; that plan for proscription was implemented in all the departments at once by the emissaries of tyranny. That is not all; draft finance bills were proposed recently that seemed to me calculated to distress the less moneyed citizens and multiply the number of malcontents. I had often unsuccessfully drawn the attention of the Committee of Public Safety to this matter; well! Would you believe that the rumour was spread that these too were my work, and that to back it up someone thought of saying that there was a finance commission in the Committee of Public Safety and that I was its chairman? But as people wanted to ruin me, especially in the opinion of the National Convention, it was claimed that I alone dared to believe that it might include a few men who were unworthy of it. Every deputy returning from a mission to the departments was told that I alone had caused him to be recalled. I was accused by very unofficial and very insinuating men of all the good and all the harm that had been done. All that I had said, and more particularly all that I had not said, was faithfully reported to my colleagues. Care was taken to remove any suspicion that anyone else had participated in any act that might have displeased someone; I had done everything, demanded everything, ordered everything; for my title of dictator should not be forgotten. [. . .]

The revolutionary Government was being rendered odious to bring about its destruction. After collecting all its orders and directing the blame for them onto those whose ruin was sought, through a veiled and universal campaign of calumnies, the revolutionary Tribunal was to be destroyed or packed with conspirators; the aristocracy called in; impunity presented to all enemies of the homeland, and the people's most zealous defenders held up to it as the authors of all the ills of the past. *If we succeed*, the conspirators said, *we will have to show extreme indulgence to draw a contrast with the present state of things*. That sentence contains the whole conspiracy. What were the crimes held against Danton, Fabre, Desmoulins? Preaching clemency for enemies of the homeland and conspiring to secure them an amnesty fatal to liberty. What would people say, if the authors of the plot I have been talking about were among those who sent Danton, Fabre and Desmoulins to the scaffold? What did the first conspirators do? Hébert, Chaumette and Ronsin[3] applied themselves to making the revolutionary Government intolerable and ridiculous, while Camille Desmoulins attacked it in satirical writings, and Fabre and Danton conspired to defend him. Some were uttering calumnies, others preparing pretexts for calumny. The same system is being operated openly today. By what stroke of fate are those who once declaimed against Hébert now defending his accomplices? How have those who declared against Danton become his imitators? How is it that those who at one time openly accused certain members of the Convention, now find themselves in league with them against the patriots whose ruin is sought? The cowards! So they wanted me to go down into the grave with ignominy! And I would have left nothing here on earth but the memory of a tyrant! How treacherously they took advantage of my good faith! How well they simulated the principles of all good citizens! How candid and affectionate was their feigned friendship! All of a sudden dark clouds veiled their faces; a fierce joy glittered in their eyes; that was the moment when they believed their measures well set to bring me down. Today they are caressing me anew; their language is more affectionate than ever; three days ago they were ready to denounce me as a Catalina;[4] today they dress me in the virtues of Cato.[5] They need some time to resume their criminal schemes. How heinous their goal is! But how contemptible their means are! Judge them by a single episode. I was asked, in the absence of one of my colleagues, to take temporary charge of a general police office, recently and poorly organized by the Committee of Public Safety. My short management ended after thirty or so decisions, some to set persecuted patriots at liberty, some to make certain of a few enemies of the Revolution. Well! Would anyone believe that that simple phrase *general police* could serve as a pretext for putting on my head the responsibility for everything done by the Committee of General Security, from the errors committed by the constituted authorities to the crimes of all our enemies? There was perhaps not one arrested individual, not one vexed citizen to whom it was not said of me: *Behold the author of your ills! You would be happy and free, were he but no more.* How could I ever list or guess all the types of impostures that were clandestinely insinuated sometimes in the National Convention, sometimes elsewhere, to render me odious or frightening? I will say only that more than six weeks ago, the nature and strength of the slander, my powerlessness to do any good or stop anything bad, forced me to relinquish absolutely my functions as a member of the Committee of Public Safety, and I swear that even in that decision I consulted only my reason and my homeland. I value my quality as a people's representative above that of member of the Committee of

Public Safety, and I put my quality as a man and French citizen before all. [. . .]

I promised some time ago to leave a testament that would be redoubtable to oppressors of the people. I am going to proclaim it now with the independence appropriate to the situation I am in: I bequeath them the dreadful truth, and death!

Representatives of the French people, it is time to resume the pride and lofty character that are proper to you. You are not made to be governed, but to govern those who place their trust in you: the tributes they owe you consist not in vain fawnings, in those flattering fables lavished on kings by ambitious ministers, but in the truth, and above all in deep respect for your principles. You have been told that all is well in the Republic: I deny it. Why did those who were warning you of frightful storms the day before yesterday see nothing yesterday but light cloud? Why do those who used to say: *I declare to you that we are walking on volcanoes*, believe today that they are walking on nothing but roses? Yesterday they believed in conspiracies; I declare that I believe in them at this very moment. Those who tell you that founding the Republic is such an easy enterprise are misleading you, or rather they cannot mislead anyone. Where are the wise institutions, where is the plan of regeneration to justify this ambitious language? Has anyone even bothered with that great project? What am I saying: was there not a wish to proscribe those who had started to prepare them? They are being praised today because people think themselves weaker: so they will be proscribed again tomorrow, if people become stronger. In four days, they say, the injustices will be put right: why were they being committed with impunity for four months? And how will the authors of all our ills be corrected or driven off in just four days? Much is said to you about your victories,[6] with a pedantic feebleness that suggests they cost our heroes neither blood nor effort: recounted less pompously, they would appear greater. It is not with rhetoricians' phrases, nor even with warlike exploits, that we will subjugate Europe, but through the wisdom of our laws, the majesty of our deliberations and the greatness of our characters. What has been done to turn our military successes to the profit of our principles, to avert the dangers of victory, or to secure us its fruits? Observe victory; observe Belgium. I warn you that your decree against the English has been violated constantly,[7] and that England, so roughly handled in our speeches, is spared by our arms. I warn you that the philanthropic comedies played by Dumouriez in Belgium are being repeated today; that people are playing about by planting sterile saplings of liberty on enemy soil, instead of gathering the fruits of victory, and that vanquished slaves are being favoured at the expense of the victorious Republic. Our enemies withdraw, and leave us to our internal divisions. Think about the end of the campaign; be afraid of internal factions; be afraid of the intrigues favoured by absence in a foreign land. Dissension has been sown among the generals, the military aristocracy is protected; loyal generals are persecuted; the military administration wraps itself in suspect authority; your decrees have been violated to loosen the yoke of the necessary supervision. These truths are as good as epigrams.

Our internal situation is much more critical. A rational financial system has yet to be created: the one in place today is paltry, spendthrift, pettifogging, ravenous and in practice absolutely independent of your overall supervision. Foreign relations are being absolutely neglected; almost all the agents employed in foreign countries, deplored for their lack of public spirit, have openly betrayed the Republic with an effrontery that still remains unpunished.

The Revolutionary Government merits your full attention: if it be destroyed today, tomorrow liberty is no more. It should not be slandered, but recalled to its principle, simplified, the numberless throng of its agents reduced, or more importantly purged: security should be provided for the people, not for its enemies. There should be no question of hobbling the people's justice through new forms; penal law ought necessarily to have something vague about it because, the current character of the conspirators being one of dissimulation and hypocrisy, justice needs to be able to grasp them in all forms. A single way of conspiring left unpunished would compromise the safety of the homeland and render it illusory. So the safeguard of patriotism lies not in the slowness or weakness of national law, but in the principles and integrity of those entrusted with it, in the good faith of the government, in the open protection it gives to patriots, and the energy with which it represses the aristocracy; in the public mind, and in certain moral and political institutions that, without hampering the workings of the law, offer a safeguard to good citizens and repress bad ones, through their influence on public opinion and on the direction of the revolutionary march; these will be proposed to you as soon as the most immediate conspiracies allow the friends of liberty time to draw breath.

Let us guide revolutionary action with wise and constantly maintained maxims; let us punish severely those who misuse revolutionary principles to vex the citizens; let people be thoroughly convinced that all those charged with national supervision, detached from any party spirit, strongly desire the triumph of patriotism and the punishment of the guilty: then everything falls into order; but if people divine that a few excessively influential men secretly want the destruction of the Revolutionary Government, that they lean towards indulgence rather than justice; if those men employ corrupt agents, if one day they slander the only authority that imposes some justice on the enemies of liberty, and the next day retract to start plotting anew; if instead of giving patriots their liberty, they give it to conspirators without distinction, then all the plotters will band together to slander patriots and oppress them. It is to these causes that the abuses should be attributed, not the Revolutionary Government, for no government exists that would not be insufferable under the same conditions.

The Revolutionary Government saved the country; it needs to be saved itself from running onto the rocks; it would be poor reasoning to believe it should be destroyed just because enemies of the public good have first paralysed it and are now doing their best to corrupt it. It is a strange way of protecting patriots, to set all the counter-revolutionaries free and make rogues triumph! It is terror of crime that makes innocence safe. [. . .]

The counter-revolution is in all parts of the political economy. The conspirators drove us despite ourselves to violent measures, rendered necessary by their crimes alone, and reduced the Republic to the most frightful scarcity, which would have starved it had it not been for the help of wholly unexpected events. That scheme was the work of foreigners, and proposed by the venal voices of the Chabots,[8] Luliers,[9] Héberts[10] and a lot of other villains. It will take all the efforts of genius to bring the Republic back to a natural and gentle system, the only one that can maintain abundance; and this work has not yet started.

We all remember the crimes committed to complete the famine pact begotten by England's infernal genius. Extracting us from that calamity took two equally unhoped-for miracles: the first was the return of our convoy sold to England before its departure from America, on which the English cabinet was counting, and the abundant and early harvest that nature presented to us; the other is the sublime patience of the people, which even put up with hunger to conserve its liberty. We still have to surmount the deficiency of labour, vehicles and horses, which is an obstacle to harvesting and the cultivation of land, and all the manoeuvres woven last year by our enemies, which they will not fail to renew.

The counter-revolutionaries have hurried here to join their accomplices, and defend their chiefs by means of plots and crimes. They are relying on imprisoned counter-revolutionaries, the people of the Vendée[11] and the deserters and enemy prisoners who, in everyone's opinion, have for some time been escaping in large numbers and coming to Paris, something I have announced several times already in the Committee of Public Safety to no avail; and lastly on the aristocracy, which is conspiring in secret all around us. Violent arguments will be provoked in the National Convention; the traitors, hitherto concealed behind hypocritical exteriors, will throw off the mask; the conspirators will accuse their accusers, and deploy all the stratagems once used by Brissot to stifle the voice of truth. If they cannot master the Convention by these means, they will divide it into two parties; and a vast field is opened for calumny and intrigue. If they gain control of it for a moment, they will accuse of despotism and resisting national authority those who fight their criminal alliance with energy; the cries of oppressed innocence, the manly accents of violated liberty will be denounced as signs of dangerous influence or personal ambition; you will think yourselves back under the knife of the former conspirators. The people will become angry; it will be called a faction; the criminal faction will continue to exasperate it, and will seek to divide the National Convention from the people; eventually it is hoped through repeated attacks to achieve disturbances, in which the conspirators will involve the aristocracy and all their accomplices to slaughter the patriots and restore tyranny. That is one part of the conspiracy's plan. And to whom should these ills be attributed? To ourselves, to our lax weakness on crime and our culpable abandonment of the principles we have proclaimed. Let us not be mistaken: establishing an immense Republic on foundations of reason and equality, holding all the parts of this immense empire together with vigorous bonds, is not an enterprise that can be completed thoughtlessly: it is the masterpiece of virtue and human reason. A host of factions springs up inside a great revolution; how can they be repressed, if you do not subject all the passions to constant justice? Your only guarantor of liberty is rigorous observation of the principles and the universal morality you have proclaimed. If reason does not reign, then crime and ambition must reign; without it, victory is just an instrument of ambition and a danger to liberty, a lethal pretext misused by intrigue to lull patriotism to sleep on the edge of the precipice; without it, what is the very meaning of victory? Victory does nothing but fortify ambition, send patriotism to sleep, awaken pride, and dig with shining hands the grave of the Republic. What does it matter if our armies drive before them the armed satellites of kings, if we retreat before the vices that destroy public liberty? What does vanquishing kings matter to us, if we are vanquished by the vices that lead to tyranny? And what have we done recently against them? We have proclaimed great principles.

What has not been done to protect them in our midst! What have we done to destroy them? Nothing, for they are raising an insolent head, and threatening virtue unpunished; nothing, for the government has retreated before the factions, and they are finding protectors among the holders of public authority; let us then expect every evil, since we are abandoning control to them. In the career we are in, to stop before the end is to perish, and we have fallen back shamefully. You have ordered the punishment of a few scoundrels responsible for all our ills; they dare to resist national justice, and the destinies of the homeland and humanity are sacrificed to them! So let us expect all the plagues that can result when factions busy themselves unpunished. Amid so many ardent passions, and in such a huge empire, the tyrants whose armies I see fleeing, but not surrounded, but not wiped out, withdraw to leave you prey to internecine dissensions which they are igniting themselves, and to an army of criminal agents you do not even know how to detect. Let go of the reins of the Revolution for a moment: you will see military despotism taking them up, and the foremost faction overthrowing the degraded national representation; a century of civil wars and calamities will desolate our homeland, and we will perish for having been unwilling to grasp a moment marked in human history for the foundation of liberty; we will deliver our homeland to a century of calamities, and the people's curses will adhere to our memory, which should have been dear to the human race! We will not even have the merit of having undertaken great things for virtuous motives; we will be confused with the unworthy people's representatives who have dishonoured national representation, and we will share their crimes by letting them go unpunished. Immortality beckoned us; and we will perish in ignominy. Good citizens will perish; bad ones will perish too; will the offended and victorious people leave them in peace to enjoy their crimes? Will not the tyrants themselves break these vile instruments? What justice have we done to the people's oppressors? What patriots oppressed by the most odious abuses of national authority have been avenged? What am I saying! Where are those who have made the voice of oppressed innocence heard, without being punished for it? Have not the culprits established the frightful principle that to denounce a disloyal representative is to conspire against national representation? The oppressor responds to the oppressed with incarceration and new insults. But do the departments in which these crimes have been committed ignore them because we forget them? And do not the complaints we reject resound with greater force in the oppressed hearts of unhappy citizens? It is so easy and so sweet to be just! Why wish the opprobrium of the guilty on ourselves by tolerating them? What! Will tolerated abuses not grow worse? Will not the guilty, if unpunished, progress from crime to crime? Do we want to share all that infamy, and condemn ourselves to the awful fate of the people's oppressors? What claim to respect do they have even from the vilest tyrants? One faction would pardon another faction; soon the villains would avenge the world by killing each other; and even if they escape human justice or their own mad rage, will they escape the eternal justice they have offended with the most horrible and heinous of all crimes?

For myself, whose very existence seems to the enemies of my country an obstacle to their odious schemes, I willingly consent to sacrifice it to them, if their frightful influence must still endure. Yes! Who could desire to see any more of that horrible succession of traitors, more or less adept at hiding their hideous souls behind a mask of virtue until such time as their crime seems ripe, and who will saddle posterity with the problem of deciding which of the enemies of my homeland was the most cowardly, the most atrocious.

If someone proposed here to announce an amnesty for perfidious deputies, and to place the crimes of any representative under the protection of a decree, a blush would appear on all our faces; but to leave loyal representatives with the duty of denouncing crimes, while exposing them on the other hand to the rage of an insolent alliance if they dare to fulfil that duty, is not that an even more revolting disorder? It is more than protecting crime; it is sacrificing virtue to it! [. . .]

People, remember that if justice does not reign with absolute authority in the Republic, and if that word does not signify love of equality and the homeland, then liberty is just a vain word! People, whom they fear, whom they flatter and despise; you who are acknowledged as sovereign, and treated as a slave, remember that where justice does not reign, the passions of magistrates do; and the people has changed its shackles, not its destiny!

Remember that there lives in your midst a league of scoundrels that struggles against public virtue, that has more influence over your affairs than you have yourself, that fears and flatters you in the mass, but proscribes you individually in the persons of all good citizens!

Remember that, instead of sacrificing this swarm of scoundrels to your well-being, your enemies want to sacrifice you to a handful of scoundrels, the authors of all our ills, and the sole obstacles to public prosperity!

Know that every man who stands up to defend your cause and public morality will be overwhelmed with rejections and proscribed by scoundrels; know that every friend of liberty will always be trapped between a duty and a calumny; that those who cannot be accused of betrayal will be accused of ambition; that the influence of probity and principle will be likened to the strength of tyranny and the violence of factions; that your trust and your esteem will be certificates of proscription for all your friends; that the cries of oppressed patriotism will be called cries of sedition, and that, not daring to attack you in the mass, they will proscribe you singly in the persons of all good citizens, until the ambitious have organized their tyranny. Such is the dominion of the tyrants armed against us, such is the influence of their alliance with corrupt men, always inclined to serve them. That then is how scoundrels are coercing us by law to betray the people, on pain of being called dictators! Shall we submit to that law? No! Let us defend the people, even at the risk of being esteemed by it; let them hurry to the scaffold by the path of crime, and us by the path of virtue.

Shall we say that all is well? Shall we continue through habit or for practicality to praise what is bad? We would ruin the homeland. Shall we expose hidden abuses? Shall we denounce traitors? They will say we are jostling the constituted authorities, that we want to acquire personal influence at their expense. So what shall we do? Our duty. What can they hold against one who wants to speak the truth and consents to die for it? So let us say that there exists a conspiracy against public liberty; that it owes its strength to a criminal coalition that intrigues inside the Convention itself; that this coalition has accomplices in the Committee of General Security and in the offices of that Committee, where they predominate; that the enemies of the Republic set that committee up against the Committee of Public Safety, thus constituting two governments; that some members of the Committee of Public Safety are in this plot; that the coalition thus formed seeks to ruin patriots and the homeland. What is the remedy to this ill? Punish the traitors, replace the staff of the Committee of General Security, purge the committee itself, constitute government unity under the supreme authority of the

National Convention, which is the centre and the judge, and in this way crush all the factions with the weight of national authority, to raise on their ruins the power of justice and liberty: such are the principles. If it is impossible to pronounce them without appearing ambitious, I would conclude that principles are proscribed and that tyranny reigns among us, but not that I should silence them; for what can they hold against a man who is right and who knows how to die for his country?

I was born to fight crime, not to control it. The time has not arrived for men of substance to be able to serve the homeland with impunity; defenders of liberty will just be outlaws, for as long as the horde of scoundrels predominates.

NOTES

INTRODUCTION

1   For a balanced historical description of the Terror, see David Andress, *The Terror. Civil War in the French Revolution*, New York: Farrar, Strauss and Giroux 2005.

2   See below, p. 115.

3   See below, p. 117.

4   Alain Badiou, *Logiques des mondes*, Paris: Seuil 2006, p. 98.

5   Louis-Antoine-Léon Saint-Just, *Oeuvres choisies*, Paris: Gallimard 1968, p. 330.

6   And he was right: as we know today, in the last days of his freedom, Louis XVI was negotiating with foreign powers a plot to start a large-scale war pitching France against the European powers, where the king would pose as a patriot, leading the French army, and then negotiate with them an honourable peace for France, thus regaining his full authority – in short, the 'gentle' Louis XVI was ready to plunge Europe into a major war in order to save his throne . . .

7   See below, p. 94.

8   See Walter Benjamin, 'Critique of Violence', in *Selected Writings*, Volume 1, 1913-1926, Cambridge (MA): Harvard University Press 1996.

9   Friedrich Engels, 'Introduction' (1891) to Karl Marx, *The Civil War in France*, in *Marx/Engels/Lenin On Historical Materialism*, New York: International Publishers 1974, p. 242.

10   See below, p. 59.

11   See below, p. 130.

12   See below, p. 43.

13   See below, p. 47.

14   See the detailed analysis in Claude Lefort, 'The Revolutionary Terror', in *Democracy and Political Theory*, Minneapolis: University of Minnesota Press 1988, pp. 50–88.

15 Claude Lefort, 'The Revolutionary Terror', in *Democracy and Political Theory*, Minneapolis: University of Minnesota Press 1988, p. 63.

16 Ibid., p. 64.

17 Ibid., p. 66.

18 Quoted from Brian Daizen Victoria, *Zen War Stories*, London: Routledge 2003, p. 132.

19 Ibid.

20 See 'The Chinese People Cannot Be Cowed by the Atom Bomb', in Mao Zedong, *On Practice and Contradiction,* introduced by Slavoj Žižek, London: Verso 2006, pp. 106–7.

21 R.R. Palmer, *Twelve Who Ruled*, New York: Atheneum 1965, p. 380.

22 See below, p. 103.

23 Margaret Washington, on: http://www.pbs.org/wgbh/amex/brown/filmmore/reference/interview/washington05.html.

24 Ibid.

25 See Henry David Thoreau, *Civil Disobedience and Other Essays*, New York: Dover Publications 1993.

26 Wendy Brown, *States of Injury*, Princeton (NJ): Princeton University Press 1995, p. 14.

27 Jean-Jacques Rousseau, *The Social Contract*, London: Penguin 2004, Book IV, Chapter 2, 'The Suffrage', p. 127.

28 Jean-Pierre Dupuy, *Petite métaphysique des tsunami*, Paris: Seuil 2005, p. 19.

29 One should bear in mind how Predestination is totally foreign to its Eastern counterpart, reincarnation. What they both share is the idea that my present state is predetermined – however, in the first case, it is by the inscrutable and contingent divine decision which precedes my existence and thus has nothing whatsoever to do with my acts, while, in the second case, it is by my own acts in my previous lives, which make my present predicament nonetheless dependent on me. What gets lost in the notion of reincarnation is the irreducible gap between virtue and grace, between my character and my fate, i.e., the utter contingency and externality of my fate with regard to my character.

30 Jacques Lacan, *The Ethics of Psychoanalysis*, London: Routledge 1992.

31 The same goes for such a radical hedonist atheist like the Marquis de Sade: perspicuous readers of his work (like Pierre Klossowski) guessed long ago that the compulsion to enjoy which drives the Sadean libertine implies a hidden reference to a hidden divinity, to what Lacan called the 'Supreme-Being-of-Evil', an obscure God demanding to be fed with the suffering of the innocents.

32 Quoted in Simon Schama, *Citizens*, New York: Viking Penguin 1989, p. 706–7.

33 See below, p. 57.

34 The trap to be avoided here is to oppose these two poles as the 'good' one versus the 'bad' one, i.e., to dismiss the institutionalized democratic procedure as the 'ossification' of the primordial democratic experience. What truly matters is precisely the degree to which the democratic explosion succeeds in getting institutionalized, translated into social order. Not only are democratic explosions easily accessible for those in power, since 'the day after' people awaken in the sober reality of power relations reinvigorated by the fresh democratic blood (which is why those in power love 'explosions of creativity' like May '68); often, the 'ossified' democratic procedure to which the majority continues to stick like a 'dead letter', is the only defence remaining against the onslaught of 'totalitarian' passions of the crowd.

35 Jacques-Alain Miller, *Le Neveau de Lacan*, Verdier 2003, p. 270.

36 Janet Afary and Kevin B. Anderson, *Foucault and the Iranian Revolution*, Chicago: The University of Chicago Press 2005, p. 263.

37 Gilles Deleuze, *Negotiations*, New York: Columbia University Press 1995, p. 171.

38 Afary and Anderson, op.cit., p. 265.

39 See Jacques Rancière, *The Politics of Aesthetics: The Distribution of the Sensible*, London: Continuum 2004.

40 Maximilien Robespierre, *Oeuvres complètes*, Paris: Ernest Leroux 1910–67, Vol. 10, p. 195.

41 See Badiou, op.cit, 'Introduction'.

42 The catch, of course, resides in the ambiguity of the 'people': are the people who are trusted the 'empirical' individuals or *the* People, on behalf of whom one can turn the terror for the people against the people's enemies into terror against individual people themselves? Does the ecological challenge not offer a unique chance to reinvent this 'eternal Idea'?

43 However, the temptation to avoid unconditionally here is to perceive ecological catastrophes themselves as a kind of 'divine violence' of nature, the justice/vengeance of nature – such a conclusion would be an unacceptable obscurantist projection of meaning into nature.

44 Ruth Scurr, *Fatal Purity*, London: Chatto & Windus 2006.

45 See *Daily Telegraph*, 6 May 2006.

46 Antonia Fraser, 'Head of the Revolution,' *The Times*, Books Section, 22 April 2006, p. 9.

47 See below, p. 129.

I ON VOTING RIGHTS FOR ACTORS AND JEWS

1 'Sur le droit de vote des comédiens et des Juifs', *Oeuvres*, vol. VI, pp. 167–8.

2 Assembly deputy and member of the upper nobility, Clermont-Tonnerre

(1757–92) was a liberal who was hostile to privileges at the beginning of the Revolution.

2 ON THE SILVER MARK

1   'Sur le Marc d'argent', *Oeuvres* vol. VII, pp. 158–74.
2   Declaration of the Rights of Man and the Citizen adopted by the Constituent Assembly in August 1789.
3   The helots were slaves in Sparta (5th century BC).
4   Aristides 'the Just' (550–467 BC): one of the strategists of the Battle of Marathon in 490 BC, a great victory of the Greeks against the Persians. Aristides was famous for his personal integrity and his reforms as *archon* of Athens that opened up the city-state's institutions to wider layers of the population.

3 ON THE CONDITION OF FREE MEN OF COLOUR

1   'Sur la condition des hommes de couleur libres', *Oeuvres* vol. VII, pp. 361–4.

4 ON THE RIGHTS OF SOCIETIES AND CLUBS

1   'Sur les droits des sociétés et des clubs', *Oeuvres* vol. VII pp. 746–8.
2   Le Chapelier (1754–1794) was one of the founders of the Jacobin Club and was the originator of the law of 14 June 1791 limiting the right of association and combination.

5 EXTRACTS FROM 'ON THE WAR'

1   'Sur la guerre' *Oeuvres*, vol. VIII, pp. 74–92.
2   Reference to the popular uprisings in the Low Countries in 1789 in the wake of the French Revolution. Strong internal contradictions obstructed the success of this movement.
3   Reference to the rallying of counter-revolutionary émigrés on the lands of the Bishop of Trier.
4   Reference to the deputy of the district of Nancy, Claude Ambroise Régnier (1746–1814).
5   Reference to Brissot's speech on 16 December 1791.

6   Reference to the replacement of Montmorin by Lessart in the Ministry of Foreign Affairs and of Duportail by Narbonne in the Ministry of War. These changes signified the victory of the bellicist faction in the king's entourage.

7   Reference to Gerville, Minister of the Interior, and Tarbé, Minister of Finance.

8   Reference to Duport du Tertre, Minister of Justice from 21 November 1790 to 22 March 1792.

9   Reference to the fact that the High Court had acquitted the counter-revolutionaries.

10   Town in the Rhineland-Palatinate which was the centre of counter-revolutionary intrigue.

11   Reference to the fact that the Minister of War, Narbonne, was then visiting the North-East frontier (which was the occasion for denunciation of the supposedly anarchic volunteer units).

6 EXTRACTS FROM 'ANSWER TO LOUVET'S ACCUSATION'

1   'Réponse à l'accusation de Louvet' (extraits), *Oeuvres* , vol. IX, pp. 79–101.

2   See Glossary.

3   Reference to Marat's organ *L'Ami du Peuple*.

4   See Glossary.

5   See Glossary.

6   See Glossary.

7   Robespierre was a member of the General Council from 10 August 1792. See Glossary.

8   Cato the Censor (234 BC–149 BC): Roman politician known for his personal austerity and opposition to luxury. A statue was built to honour him but several times his enemies raised the populace against him.

9   The surveillance committee was one of the committees of the Commune which was in charge of the revolutionary police. It directed the purges of September 1793 with the help of the 'Law of Suspects'.

10   Reference to the accusation of illegality that Clodius directed at Cicero when the latter broke the coup d'état led by Catalina at the end of the Roman Republic (first century BC).

11   Reference to the suppression of royalist newspapers such as l'*Ami du Roi* after 10 August 1792.

12   Reference to the 'September Massacres' of 1792. In a context of the danger of an invasion there was a massacre in Paris of a number of prisoners, especially of priests and nobles.

13   Reference to the Brunswick Manifesto of 25 July 1792, which threatened

Paris with 'exemplary vengeance' should the slightest harm be done to the royal family.

14 Danton then gave his famous speech against the 'enemies of the *patrie*': 'To defeat them, we will need audacity, yet more audacity, always more audacity [*il nous faut de l'audace, encore de l'audace, toujours de l'audace*], and France is saved.'

15 See Glossary.

16 Originally composed of bourgeois men and led by La Fayette, the composition of the National Guard became more heteroclite with time. It was then at the heart of the divisions between revolutionary currents.

17 During the summer of 1792, battalions of *Fédérés* streamed towards the capital to save Paris from the attacks of the coalition forces.

18 Instituted on 21 October 1789, martial law was firmly opposed by Robespierre. It was abolished by the Convention on 23 June 1793.

19 Reference to *La Sentinelle*, Louvet's anti-royalist poster-newspaper, which had started on 1 March 1792.

20 Close to Marie-Antoinette and the counter-revolution, the Princesse de Lamballe fell victim to the September Massacres.

21 Former Minister of Foreign Affairs for Louis XVI, killed in the September Massacres.

22 One of the main leaders of the aristocratic emigration, Condé left France after the storming of the Bastille (14 July 1789).

7 EXTRACTS FROM 'ON SUBSISTENCE'

1 'Sur les subsistances' (extraits), *Oeuvres*, vol. IX, pp. 110–20.

2 See also the text 'Draft Declaration of the Rights of Man and of the Citizen pp. 111-171.

3 Reference to Turgot and the 1774 edict on trade and grain which sparked off the 'Flour Wars'. Turgot resigned and was replaced by Necker.

4 Tantalus was the mythical king of Lydia, condemned to live tortured by thirst and hunger.

8 ON THE TRIAL OF THE KING

1 'Sur le jugement du roi', *Oeuvres*, vol. IX, pp. 120–30.

2 Reference to the trial of King Charles I in 1649 during the English Revolution in which Cromwell played a leading role.

3   Reference to the trial of Mary Stuart by Elizabeth I, Queen of England, in 1587. She was condemned to death for the Catholic plot she had supposedly orchestrated.
4   Tarquin the Proud was the last king of Rome before the Republic. Having been chased out of power by the people, he sought refuge with the tyrant of Cumae (509 BC).
5   Pétion proposed to the Convention that Louis XVI be judged by the Assembly.
6   Reference to the attacks of the Girondins against the legitimacy of the overthrow of the king on 10 August 1792.

9 DRAFT DECLARATION OF THE RIGHTS OF MAN AND OF THE CITIZEN

1   'Projet de déclaration des droits de l'homme et du citoyen', *Oeuvres*, vol. IX, pp. 457–70.
2   This is a reference to the expression 'agrarian law', borrowed from ancient Rome, to sow distrust against those calling for the division of property. On 18 March 1793, the Convention decreed the death penalty for those who called for such measures.
3   Fabricius was a Roman Consul (third century BC) celebrated by his compatriots for his disinterested nature and the austerity of his lifestyle.
4   Crassus (first century BC): Roman general and politician notorious his personal enrichment at the expense of proscribed citizens.
5   See note 5 of chapter 2, in this volume.
6   In ancient Greece the Prytaneum was an important building used for political and religious purposes.
7   Xerxes: ruler of Persia from 485 to 465 BC, defeated at Salamis (480 BC) after having ruined Athens.
8   The French royal dynasty.
9   See Glossary.

10 EXTRACTS FROM 'IN DEFENCE OF THE COMMITTEE OF PUBLIC SAFETY AND AGAINST BRIEZ'

1   'Pour la défense du comité de salut public et contre Briez', *Oeuvres,* vol. X, pp. 116–25.
2   Houchard and Landremont, commanders of the armies of the North and the Rhine, were removed from their posts on 24 September.

3 Houchard took the town of Hondschoote on 8 September 1793 but was accused of treason for having let the coalition armies escape; he was condemned by the tribunal and guillotined on 16 November 1793.

4 Jourdan (1762–1833): a general in 1793, he distinguished himself at the battle of Hondschoote in September 1793. He was also behind the decisive battle of Fleurus on 26 June 1794 which opened Belgium up to the French forces.

5 Manuel-Louis Ernoult was appointed brigadier general on 20 September 1793.

6 Reference to William Pitt the Younger (1759–1806), the British Prime Minister.

7 The *Marais* [swamp or marshland] refers to the moderate centre of the Convention, oscillating between the Girondins and the Montagnards.

8 General Custine (1740–93) won many important victories and was appointed Chief of the Army of the North in May 1793. But after the fall of Mayence he was accused of treason and condemned to death.

9 Lamarlière: Chief of Staff of the Army of the Ardennes in March 1793, removed in July, condemned to death and executed in November.

II EXTRACTS FROM 'REPORT ON THE POLITICAL SITUATION OF THE REPUBLIC'

1 'Rapport sur la situation politique de la République', *Oeuvres*, vol. X, pp. 167–84.

2 See Glossary.

3 Champ-de-Mars : under the impetus of the Cordelier Club, a petition was presented calling for the deposition of the king and another one calling for his trial. The latter was laid on the altar of the Champ-de-Mars. Martial law was proclaimed and the National Guards, under the command of La Fayette, fired on the crowd. The incident accentuated the divisions between members of the Assembly.

4 Nancy: reference to the repression of the mutiny of the Swiss Guards of Châteauvieux in August 1790.

5 Reference to the Girondins who, according to Robespierre, had exploited the enthusiasm of the popular societies in order to push for war.

6 See the speech 'On the War'.

7 In early 1793.

8 After Valmy, Dumouriez had allowed the Prussians to escape, refraining from imposing a definitive defeat on them. See Glossary.

9 Reference to the division plan at the Anvers conference of 1793 which fixed the war aims of the coalition forces.

10   The Prince of Orange-Nassau was the real ruler of Holland inasmuch as he was captain and admiral general of the United Provinces.

11   Joseph II and Leopold: the two Germanic emperors who reigned successively from 1765 to 1790 and then 1790 to 1792.

12   Maria-Theresa: Empress who ruled Austria from 1740 to 1780.

13   Catherine II, empress of Russia from 1762 to 1796.

14   Reference to the second partition of Poland (23 January 1793).

15   The Genoan Republic was at this time independent.

16   Reference to Bernstorff, the enlightened Danish Minister of Foreign Affairs, who refused to join the coalition against France.

17   King of the Mycenaeans who accompanied his troops in the siege of Troy.

18   The Duke of Södermanland, successor to Gustav III who died on 16 March 1792. He established closer links with France.

19   Reference to the Prussian monarchy.

20   Huns: people of Asiatic origin who ravaged part of Europe at the end of antiquity.

21   Tartars: people of Mongol descent who occupied Russia in the thirteenth century.

22   Murder of Julius Caesar in 44 BC.

23   On 29 August 1793 the royalists handed Toulon over to the English. The Republican army took it back on 19 December.

24   Brigand in an Aventine cave who was slain by Hercules.

12 RESPONSE OF THE NATIONAL CONVENTION TO THE MANIFESTOS OF THE KINGS ALLIED AGAINST THE REPUBLIC

1   'Réponse de la Convention nationale aux manifestes des rois ligués contre la République', *Oeuvres,* vol. X, pp. 226–33.

2   Roman emperor (14–37 AD) referred to here due to his reputation for cruelty and hypocrisy.

3   Roman emperor (41–54 AD) referred to here because he was dominated and then poisoned by his wife Agrippina.

4   George III, king of Great Britain (1760–1820), who suffered from mental illness.

5   Valeria Messalina (20–48 AD), Roman empress notorious for her sexual promiscuity.

6   Marie-Antoinette, queen of France, executed on 16 October 1793.

7   See note 4 of chapter 8, this volume.

8   Etruscan king at the end of the sixth century BC who wished to reinstall the dynasty of the Tarquins.

9 Mucius Scaevola (end of sixth century BC): legendary Roman hero who, during the war against the Etruscans, slipped into the enemy camp in order to kill Porsena. Imprisoned by the Etruscans, he let his right hand be burnt in the fire rather than denounce his accomplices.

10 See note 7 of chapter 9, this volume.

11 See note 4 of chapter 2, this volume.

12 Octavian, Antony and Lepidus: triumvirate who shared power in the Roman Republic after Caesar's death (44 BC).

13 Sejanus (20BC–31 AD): Emperor Tiberius's praetorian prefect.

14 Brutus and Cassius: the assassins of Julius Caesar.

15 Reference to Jean-Baptiste Drouet, deputy in the Convention, imprisoned by the Austrians at the end of October 1793.

16 Baille (Pierre Marie, 1750–93) and Beauvais (Charles Nicolas Beauvais de Préau, 1745–94): two *représentants en mission* sent to Toulon by the Convention and imprisoned by the royalists in July 1793. Baille committed suicide in prison and Beauvais died a few months after his liberation.

17 Gasparin: *représentant en mission*, killed in the town of Orange on 11 November 1793.

13 ON THE PRINCIPLES OF REVOLUTIONARY GOVERNMENT

1 'Sur les principes du gouvernement révolutionnaire', *Oeuvres*, vol. X, pp. 273–82.

2 See 'Revolutionary Goverment' in Glossary.

3 Toulon was taken back from the English on 19 December 1793.

4 The latter is a reproach vis-à-vis the 'ultra-revolutionaries', especially for their policy of 'dechristianization'.

5 Reference to Anarcharsis Cloots who was called 'the orator of the human race' and whom Robespierre criticized for his 'atheist' positions.

6 See note 11 of chapter 5, this volume.

7 Themistocles : Athenian magistrate who won the Battle of Salamis against the Persians (480 BC).

8 Scipio Africanus defeated Hannibal in 202 BC and captured Cathage, Rome's great rival.

9 See Glossary.

10 See Glossary.

11 Reference to Collot d'Herbois and Fouché who had repressed anti-revolutionary activity in Lyons; Fouché was accused of excesses.

12 See Glossary.

13 See note 9 of chapter 10, this volume.

14 See Glossary.
15 Baron de Dietrich (1748–93): supporter of a constitutional monarchy, he tried to raise Strasbourg in revolt after 10 August 1792 before emigrating; on his return he was condemned to death and guillotined.
16 Biron, Armand Louis de Gontaut (1747–93): a liberal noble, he held a number of military posts before being accused of a lack of enthusiasm by the Convention; he was condemned and guillotined in July 1793.
17 Brulys (Ernault de Bignac des) 1757–1809: Chief of Staff of the three armies of the North, Belgium and the Ardennes in April 1793. Suspended in August 1793, arrested and imprisoned, he was only released after the fall of Robespierre. Barthélémy (François de) 1747–1830: French ambassador to the Swiss cantons 1792 to 1797.

14 ON THE PRINCIPLES OF POLITICAL MORALITY THAT SHOULD GUIDE THE NATIONAL CONVENTION IN THE DOMESTIC ADMINISTRATION OF THE REPUBLIC

1 'Sur les principes de morale politique qui doivent guider la Convention nationale dans l'administration intérieure de la République', *Oeuvres*, vol. X pp. 350–66.
2 The Ventôse decrees were supposed to sequester the goods of the 'enemies of the revolution' and share them out among the poor; they had only begun to be applied before they were cut short.
3 Roman historian (55–120 AD).
4 Philosopher and politician of the Renaissance (1469–1527).
5 Tiberius and Vespasian: Roman emperors (14–37 AD) and (69–79 AD).
6 Lycurgus : mythical Spartan legislator (ninth century BC).
7 Agis: king of Sparta in the fourth century BC who tried to restore Lycurgus's laws.
8 Demosthenes was the Athenian leader (384–322 BC) who led the resistance against the Macedonian king, Philip.
9 Miltiades (540–489 BC): Athenian general who was commander at the Battle of Marathon (490 BC) against the Persians.
10 See note 5 of chapter 2, this volume.
11 See chapter 6, p. 42.
12 Caesar, Piso, Clodius : rival chiefs competing for power at the end of the Roman Republic (first century BC).
13 Reference to Anarcharsis Cloots; see note 5 of chapter 13, this volume.
14 Caligula and Heliogabalus: Roman emperors notorious for their great cruelty (37–41 and 218–222 AD).

15 Reference to Fabre d'Eglantine (1750–94), implicated in the French East India Company Affair (see Glossary) and arrested on 12 January 1794.

15 EXTRACTS FROM SPEECH OF 8 THERMIDOR YEAR II

1 'Discours du 26 juillet 1794 / 8 thermidor an II', (extraits) *Oeuvres*, vol. X pp. 542–76.
2 See note 4 of chapter 7, this volume.
3 See Glossary.
4 See note 10 of chapter 6, this volume.
5 See note 8 of chapter 6, this volume. Cato the Younger supported Cicero against Catalina; he killed himself in 46 BC.
6 Reference to Carnot and Barère who tried to take the credit for the Republic's military victories.
7 Reference to a decree of Autumn 1793 to confiscate all the English goods acquired in France.
8 Chabot, François (1756–94): an important figure in the Cordelier Club, deputy to the Convention, was condemned and guillotined for his involvement in the East India Company affair (see Glossary).
9 Lulier, Louis Marie (1746–94): member of the Commune, he was arrested during the trial of the Hébertists; he was acquitted but he committed suicide in prison.
10 See Glossary.
11 See Glossary.